DADDY ISSUES

How to Detangle From the Sins of Our Fathers

CHRISTIAN JACKSON

Contents

Introduction

"That's messed up!" I was shouting at the top of my lungs at my supervisor...and I may or may not have used a stronger word. This man was writing me up for supposedly changing the climate of a work meeting that we were having the week before.

He stared at me. Blank faced. I was in just as much shock as he was.

"You know what I've been through with this place and you literally come to me with something as dumb as this?! If you write me up, it better be for punching someone in the face!" I was livid.

He insisted that my playful eye roll in response to something he said was inhibiting the work progress on the new protocol that he was, frankly, making up for no reason and, thus, adding to the work we already did. I know. It's not the way you behave when you speak to your superior at work. It's not graceful. It's not professional. It's not me. But the year before this conversation taught me to assert myself the way I never learned. Needless to say, my delivery could have used a little tweaking.

I had never been bullied by an authority figure with so much influence. Despite this, the feeling was familiar. After that meeting, I realized how much working with this man sitting across from me triggered insecurities I had for a long time. Let me back up...

I'm Christian Jackson, a Licensed Professional Counselor and Certified Addictions Counselor in the state of South Carolina. I earned a bachelor's degree in psychology and a master's of science degree in Mental Health Counseling from Winthrop University, completing practicums, volunteering with under-served populations, and developing programs on many scales that were designed to help others.

I spent the last 10 years amassing the formal education and training to offer trauma-specific treatment to my clients that addresses their diagnoses. I worked as a therapist for clients from myriad backgrounds, expanding beyond the therapist role to facilitating community outreach and educating people about mental health.

These accolades are not usually connected with the occasional "F-Bomb" toward one's superior. But we all have an origin story, and mine had its share of struggles.

Despite my accomplishments, I was terrified of entrepreneurship. I thought there was too much liability. I didn't want to be responsible for so much. And, mostly, I didn't think I would be successful. These were glaring self-esteem symptoms, the product of my own unresolved Daddy Issues, or DI.

My father never told me I couldn't accomplish things, but he didn't tell me I could, either. He was and is pretty critical. When I was very young, we used to play a game where I made up inventions and told him all about the products I had dreamed up. I felt smart and empowered that he took an interest in my thoughts.

At some point, though, he seemed to stop believing in my ideas...and me.

When Daddy told me to do something, I sometimes had a question--just a child's curiosity. His response was swift: I was to do as I was told, no questions asked. It didn't take long to learn I needed to shut up or feel the wrath. This is likely where my "not good enough" narrative was born.

I remember reading a *Seventeen* magazine once at my grandmother's hair salon. The experience in the salon could take hours, especially as a non-paying family member. I had to get in where she could fit me, bobbing and weaving (no pun intended) between her scheduled appointments. This was before the days of zoning out on a cellphone, scrolling timelines, and I looked forward to reading the newest magazines on the coffee table to pass the time. Daddy walked in, saw what I was reading and snatched it out of my hand.

"Are you seventeen?" he asked.

"No..." I was legitimately confused. The tone of his voice still rings in my head. He wasn't happy.

"Then whatchu think you doin'?" It was rhetorical, of course. He didn't really care to hear my response and I dared not give one. Looking back, I suppose he was trying to dictate what was appropriate for his 12-year-old to be exposed to. But the guy loved to put on a show. He embarrassed my brother and me countless times with statements or productions like this when he had an audience.

In private, my dad would overtly show his disdain when things didn't go his way, yelling, scoffing and exhibiting passive-aggressive behaviors. Watching the interactions between him and my mother stunted my knowledge of how to articulate my feelings in a healthy way. Instead, I learned:

1. Your opinion matters only a little, if at all.
2. You're not the boss of your life.
3. You have to work harder to be heard.
4. Your best isn't good enough.

These "lessons" repeated themselves at critical junctions in my personal relationships and my career. Each time, I felt the need for my father's approval and the shame of failure when situations did not work out the way I hoped--even at times when I went months or longer without speaking to him. I could hear him in my head, dictating what I should have done. Despite my attempts to push through, negative thoughts spiraled, born out of those pesky rules I learned as a child. I criticized myself harshly. *What would your dad say if he saw you now? He told you you would fail. Where did you learn to make decisions, anyway?*

I have been working since I was 16 and was always a good employee, and now enjoy a career to which I believe I was called. I am a rule follower to the T most times. Not because of my integrity, but because I am afraid of the consequences. It is difficult to navigate developing a healthy opinion when I wasn't allowed to voice or even really have one.

When I'm told "no" or that I have to jump through many hoops to help someone, I feel a twinge in my spirit. I can see Daddy's face in those moments, as if he is the one denying housing for a client who is not yet 30 days clean. Throw in the many injustices against women and racial discrimination in work settings and whew! There are layers on layers. I have to fight becoming the little girl who was discouraged from going the extra mile. The "What's the point" narrative rears its head.

I wrote this book to help women like me unpack the symptoms and the roots of their Daddy Issues. We don't have to be trapped in the distortions in which we were raised. Therefore, it's important for us to find ways to exercise our separate, beautifully unique voices in the workplace and our personal lives.

I've been in positions where I'm grinding, desperately seeking the approval I didn't get from a father who decided not to take interest. It took time to find a balance between being the overachiever who sought a pat on the back because she was deprived of that and becoming a woman confident enough to speak her piece.

You're enough, no matter how your DI manifests. If you're a woman with DI, you may have heard the critical voice of your father or tried to compensate for his absence. You may have struggled to avoid letting him down, because the pressure of his expectations was overwhelming.

Regardless of where you fall on the spectrum, it's high time we reclaim the vision God has for us. We were knit together with a purpose before we were born. Our Heavenly Father knew you would have the trial you just endured. You've been equipped all along. He knew you would win despite the kicking and screaming you did along the way. He can't wait to use what you perceive as an imperfection. These truths are crucial to hang on to.

It's amazing really, that God sees us in a way we can't even perceive sometimes. So, hold your head high the next time you enter a meeting. You can lead in ways you probably don't realize.

I mentioned earlier that life taught me things, like it does for all of us. The more I started to sit with people in their pain, the more I realized I needed to unload some of the lessons from my sessions! It's important you know that I've been on the other side of the couch. Don't get it twisted, therapists need therapy, too. In fact, I believe it is responsible for us to do our own work when pouring into our clients' lives.

This wouldn't be possible without me following through on acknowledging, learning from, and accepting the pain of dealing with my Daddy Issues. And sis, I can't wait to tell you how freeing it is!

ONE

What to Expect

This is not your average self-help manual. You may experience raw emotions...just as I did while writing the book. I say bad words, reveal my own pettiness at times, because I am imperfect but honest in my self assessment and I want you to be comfortable doing the same.

I am not a Christian therapist, but I am a therapist who is a Christian. I mention God's help throughout the book because this would not be my authentic voice and experience without it. I want you to know I honor your tradition, whether it be Christian, Muslim, Jewish, Indigenous, Eastern, or no doctrine at all. My point rests on the idea that when you make a step toward your own power, that energy gathers and works for your own good.

I want you to feel like we are kicking it while getting your hair braided by a best friend. Because, Sis, I've got some tea. I have a little bit for my younger sisters and my elders. I want this to spark conversations between people, and I want you to release. The goal is for you to develop personal methods to make connections between your thoughts and emotions when you are triggered.

You may come across things that you don't like. Great. Do something about it. Daddy issues are not easy ones to address. I am so thankful to have come out on the other side and found what closure looks like for me. I am optimistic about your future! My hope is that this book will help you face the hard stuff and speak truth to the lies that may have derived from your Daddy Issues.

But first, let's see where you stand with taking care of your needs. At the end of each chapter is a self-care assessment or worksheet aimed at helping you process what you may have learned about yourself. It's a good idea to have a notebook or digital document dedicated solely to this process. Let's get started.

TWO

Self-Care Assessment

How well do you take care of your mental, physical, spiritual, and emotional well being? This initial read is called a baseline, where we will ascertain your natural habits. If your score is low, don't be hard on yourself. This is not a test or a quiz, this is a roadmap. Knowing where you are helps point you in the proper direction for growth!

USING THE SCALE BELOW, rate the following areas in terms of frequency:

5= Yea, girl. All the time
4= I do, mostly!
3= Um, sometimes.
2= Not really.
1=Nah, sis. I don't even think of it.

Mental Self-Care
I go to therapy
I go to support groups
I set healthy boundaries
I watch and listen to positive messages (ie podcasts, books, shows, music, etc.)
I write in a journal
I know when I am overwhelmed
I have a set of 3 or more healthy coping skills I use regularly
I have fun, healthy hobbies outside of work and other responsibilities
I take time off when necessary
I have a self-care routine

Physical Self-Care
I have a primary care physician
I have annual check-ups
I eat regularly
I watch what I eat
I drink water
I get enough rest
I keep up with my appearance
I have a good, healthy hygiene routine
I engage in physical activity
I minimize alcohol/drug use

Spiritual Self-Care
I go to a place of worship

I practice reverence in my home
I pray or meditate
I listen to positive spiritual messages
I reflect on myself (ie decisions, plans, hurts,
successes, etc.)
I use positive affirmations
I have spiritual mentors or friends
I spend time in nature
I practice yoga or other mind-body systems
I share my truth in safe spaces with safe people

Emotional Self-Care
I know when I'm emotionally overwhelmed
I cry
I laugh
I allow myself to be vulnerable
I express myself in healthy ways
I check in with myself (ie, "are you ok, sis?")
I have positive self-talk
I know triggers for both positive and negative
emotions
I have a positive, upright posture
I am engaged in my community

SCORE YOURSELF PER SECTION; the highest possible
score in each is a 50.

0-20=Let's work; time to start considering yourself.
21-40=Alright, we're on the way...

40+=Keep up the good work, sis!

Now that you have an idea of what you are already doing, or not doing, for yourself, take a look at this self-care outline. It will help you make declarations for your holistic health. It is complete with measurable ways to track your intentional self-care regimen with mental, physical, emotional, and spiritual considerations. It will help inform the ways you address the issues you have identified. The Self-Care Diamond that follows will provide suggestions of healthy activities for each area. Check this out.

THREE

Self-Care Outline

I can improve my **mental** health by...

I will do at least 2 things on the self care diamond/list by [insert date]

I will know I am improving when [insert how you know you are making strides]

I will reward myself by [insert one of your favorite treats]

Complete example: *I can improve my mental health by starting a journal and taking time off from work. I will schedule one day off a month. I will know I am making progress when I notice that I am getting better at knowing what contributes to my anxiety. I will reward myself by taking a walk.*

I can improve my **physical** health by

I will do at least 2 things on this list by [insert date]

I will know I am better when [insert how you know you are making strides]

I will reward myself by [insert one of your favorite treats]

Complete example: *I can improve my physical health by making an appointment with my primary care physician and drinking more water. I will set a doctor's appointment within the next two weeks. I will know I am making progress when I notice that I actually went to the appointment with my primary care physician. I will reward myself by eating a healthy snack.*

I can improve my **emotional** health by

I will do at least 2 things on this list by [insert date]

I will know I am better when [insert how you know you are making strides]

I will reward myself by [insert one of your favorite treats]

Complete example: *I can improve my emotional health by setting boundaries with unhealthy people and noticing where my negative emotions land in my body. I will calmly speak my truths this week. I will know I am making progress when I notice that I am taking more time for myself. I will reward myself by watching my favorite, uplifting TV show.*

I can improve my **spiritual** health by...

I will do at least 2 things on this list by [insert date]

I will know I am better when [insert how you know you are making strides]

I will reward myself by [insert one of your favorite treats]

Complete example: *I can improve my spiritual health by spending at least one day in nature and writing affirmations for myself. I will know I am making progress when I notice that I am having at least one less anxious or depressed thought a day. I will reward myself by expressing gratitude to my spiritual root.*

FOUR

Self-Care Diamond

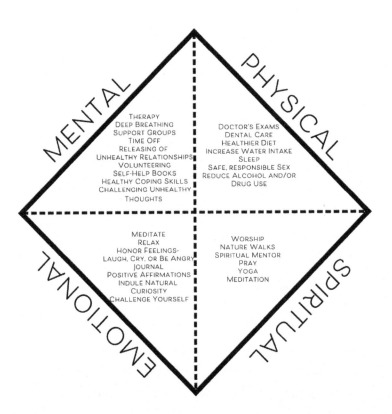

MENTAL

PHYSICAL

THERAPY
DEEP BREATHING
SUPPORT GROUPS
TIME OFF
RELEASING OF
UNHEALTHY RELATIONSHIPS
VOLUNTEERING
SELF-HELP BOOKS
HEALTHY COPING SKILLS
CHALLENGING UNHEALTHY
THOUGHTS

DOCTOR'S EXAMS
DENTAL CARE
HEALTHIER DIET
INCREASE WATER INTAKE
SLEEP
SAFE, RESPONSIBLE SEX
REDUCE ALCOHOL AND/OR
DRUG USE

MEDITATE
RELAX
HONOR FEELINGS-
LAUGH, CRY, OR BE ANGRY
JOURNAL
POSITIVE AFFIRMATIONS
INDULE NATURAL
CURIOSITY
CHALLENGE YOURSELF

WORSHIP
NATURE WALKS
SPIRITUAL MENTOR
PRAY
YOGA
MEDITATION

EMOTIONAL

SPIRITUAL

Mental: Therapy; deep breathing; support groups; time off; releasing unhealthy relationships; volunteering; self-help books; healthy coping skills; challenging unhealthy thoughts
Physical: Doctor's exams; dental care; healthier diet; regular exercise; increase water intake; sleep; safe, responsible sex; reduce alcohol and/or drug use
Emotional: Meditate; relax; honoring feelings--cry, laugh, or be angry; journal; positive affirmations; indulge natural curiosity; challenge yourself
Spiritual: Worship; nature walk; spiritual mentor; pray; yoga; meditation

FIVE

What are Daddy Issues Anyway?

I make bold observations when I'm facilitating therapy. It's part of how I practice.

I BUILD rapport with the client, we laugh and talk about things that interest them. We may even have things in common. There is a hilarious meme that says *"When your therapist does that thing where they open a session talking about pizza and somehow you end up revealing your trauma."* I'm that therapist.

I STORE the information for a future session so we can pull on it to make things light when we get to processing some hard truths. I believe in telling a client what I think their diagnosis is. It could be bipolar disorder. Major depression. Generalized anxiety disorder. Adjustment disorder. A whole gamut of substance use disorders. We go over the symptoms and come up with a plan to manage the overwhelming emotions. I normalize it because I believe in educating throughout the process; this way, the person is able to identify what relates to them and start the work. And because of the relationship we have built up front, telling my clients their diagnoses hasn't been a problem.

OF COURSE, there are a few occasions when this doesn't go well. Some diagnoses are a little touchy. When I tell someone they have Daddy Issues, they look like I've told them they have two heads. It can feel offensive to be told one has issues tracing back to their father. This may be because the person completely denounced their father, so mentioning him activates something uncomfortable. They've likely put that relationship in a compartment far away. Other times people idealize their parental relationships and think I've somehow blasphemed dear old dad. It's time to flesh out the definition of Daddy Issues; what does it even mean?

NOW, Daddy Issues is not a diagnosis you will find in the *Diagnostic and Statistical Manual of Mental Disorders, Fifth Edition* (DSM-5). It's something I made up with scripture in mind. The V-code in parentheses is based on Romans 8:16-17 (16. *The Spirit himself testifies with our spirit that we are God's children. 17. Now if we are children, then we are heirs---heirs of God and coheirs with Christ, if indeed we share in his sufferings in order that we may also share in his glory*-NIV).

IN ORDER TO BREAK CYCLES, we have to know where we stand. Symptoms of DI try to derail the fact that we all have purpose, no matter how we feel or what we have been told about ourselves. Grace enhances this notion that much more. We must be able to combat the negative self-talk with truth. Maybe that's a mantra or an affirmation. It could be a friend who speaks to you with love. Either way, we have to arm ourselves with something positive; I choose God's word every time. And I find it in music, podcasts, nature, television, you name it!

Another part of the inspiration for this very real, yet unofficial, diagnosis is based on reactive attachment and separation anxiety disorders from the DSM-5. Check it; I present to you, our working definition of DI (V16.17) ...

Diagnostic Criteria:

A. The physical and/or emotional absence to overbearing physical and/or emotional presence of a father that results in at least one of the following:

    1. Feelings and/or thoughts of abandonment
    2. Feelings and/or thoughts of worthlessness
    3. Confusion and/or difficulty making decisions

B. The presence of a father where the relationship was unhealthy. This may result in one or more of the following:

    1. Extreme stress
    2. Inability to trust one's own judgment
    3. Feelings and/or thoughts of inadequacy

C. The person has experienced consistent trouble manifesting healthy relationships. This applies to familial, professional, *intimate, and parenting relationships (must appear in at least one of these categories).*

D. *The doubt, shame, abandonment, anxiety, and/or depression is persistent to some degree, lasting at least 6 weeks in children and adolescents and at least 3 months for adults.*

E. *The disturbance causes clinically significant distress in multiple areas of one's life, evident in one's behavior.*

IN ORDER TO meet a full diagnosis of DI, one must meet at least three of these symptoms following exposure to a father on the spectrum of physically/emotionally absent to overbearingly present physically/emotionally. I want you to see how this will apply to the majority. It's not hard to meet criteria for DI because again, no one can escape family patterns. We are the products of our family's dysfunction. By reading this book, you are going to be equipped with how to break the generational cycle. It can start with you. You won't be perfect, but you will have made connections to do better. Now that we have a framework, how do we trace this back?

FAMILY OF ORIGIN

Family of Origin, or FOO, is a clinical term that describes the village of people who had an influence on our formative years. They are the people who raised us; more specifically, the people we likely lived with. It is so crucial to grasp this concept as we begin outlining what DI means. This place is the core of our development. It's where we learned how to walk and talk. We picked up morals, values, and spirituality. It's where we learned how to interact with others. This place is the breeding ground for how to process emotions...or avoid them.

Think of the people who raised you. Were they kind? Supportive? Absent? Critical? These interactions are learned. They shape the self-talk we have and our worldview, which then drives the resulting emotions and feelings.

My mother and father married straight out of high school. They had my brother and me soon after. Imagine these kids, my parents, trying to raise two babies at 19 and 20 years old. I'm told there were nights we ate "onion soup," a creation my dad came up with when there was no food. There was a clear struggle in providing physical needs; thankfully, we ended up alright.

My earliest memories include more than the struggle. I remember going to the mall dressed alike; we all wore denim on denim...it was the 90s. I thought that was so cool! I was never an outside girl, but going to the park from time to time was fun. We were at church a lot; Daddy was a youth pastor and was dynamic with at-risk youth. I so admired that about him. I learned the value of hard work watching him grind. I learned selflessness from my mother. There weren't many sit-down, impactful conversations about how to deal with life, but my brother and I watched pretty closely and used my parents' actions as our lessons.

There were also the times my parents argued. I never knew what it was for, but I remember Mommy being so mad she would storm out of the house, slamming the door. My brother and I wondered when or if she would come back. Those nights were devastating. Daddy was clearly dominant. Looking back, I'm quite sure his authoritarian attitude is what got to her the most.

She's always been sensitive, in tune with the overwhelming emotions she felt. Daddy never physically abused my mother, but the verbal jabs toward her were ever present.

My mom always had a way of standing out. Her curvy frame sits at about five feet flat with a personality way bigger. I swear, that woman doesn't care what comes out of her mouth! She was my first style icon, always dressed in a way that expressed what she wanted to say even when she didn't utter a word. She was so fly. To this day, she can stop a room with her radiance.

It was something I didn't always appreciate growing up. After all, it's ok to have the "cool mom", but the one all your guy friends crushed on? It wasn't long before my brother's friends were referring to her as Ms. Parker, the sexy woman who watered her lawn in daisy dukes in the movie *Friday*. I borrowed her clothes all the time as a budding young woman. I played with her lipstick colors and borrowed her jewelry. I even pushed the limits when I really wanted to impress a boy and wore a pair of her high heeled stilettos to school when she had already told me to leave them alone...fell flat on my face that day!

She wore her hair in a natural cut, before it was cool to wear our bald fades and curly fros again. She grew it out, styled it in small puffs, and colored it blonde. After more than 20 years, she decided to switch up her look and now rocks a fiery red fro with a hint of blonde, for the ombre feel. Mommy loved trying new things and expressing herself through art. She sang in the choir at church and was on the praise team too, doing a little two step to "Our God is an Awesome God." Everyone at church knew who she was, not only because she was the youth pastor's wife, but because her spirit is infectious and leaves you uplifted.

Because of our 20-year age difference, it was like having a big sister who loved me like no other. I wanted to be like her because she was so unapologetic about her styling choices, advice, and the way she mothered my brother and me. We felt seen when we sat with her. That smile hit you and the world was better. Even the "Mom Look" (the death-stare, side eye) was inspired by loving correction, not negative judgment.

But watching Mommy interact with Daddy revealed a duality in her existence. The radiance she showed the world was her way of putting on a mask of her own. At home, I could tell how hard she tried to stand her ground, yet please her husband. The two didn't seem to go together. Mommy's outgoing personality attracted attention Daddy didn't appreciate. He obviously married the wrong one: she certainly wasn't a wallflower.

When her personality or her parenting choices clashed with his, Daddy would shut it down. He undermined her authority and spoke to her like she was a child. I remember him talking to other people about how Mommy "couldn't sing." I'm not even sure what could have prompted his jab other than someone complimenting her. It was hard to hear him tell other family members or friends something so hurtful about her gift. She stopped singing for a while. Turns out word got back to her. I studied their exchanges, wondering if this is what a marriage was. I was only a kid, but I knew they were supposed to have each other's backs at the very least. This didn't feel right.

"What are you stressed out about?" Daddy said one day. He was in the Air Force, and we had been stationed in Albuquerque for a few months. I don't recall what they were arguing about, but Mommy was upset, crying.

"Why are you worried about it? When you stress, it stresses the whole family out!" And that was it. Mommy left the room. My brother and I just watched. Looking back, I'm quite sure that could have been more productive if he asked her what was wrong, empathized. A bit of reassurance would have gone a long way. But that's not how things went down in the Ray household.

As I grew to adulthood, Mommy opened up more about the impact of being married to Daddy. She shared how she supported him in his endeavors. There were several trials and errors Daddy made trying to find his way in the business world. His failures weren't handled with much grace, but my mom was there every step, pushing him along. Eventually, the lack of appreciation, verbal abuse and overall pressure led to the demise of their relationship. She decided there was no reason to continue respecting and honoring her husband anymore, which led to her doing her own thing, if you catch my drift. It's not something she is proud of, but what do you do when you're a woman with your own DI and still searching to be loved in your marriage? It's not always a pretty picture.

Can you guess the messages I took away? From watching my parents marriage, I knew that someday my own husband would respect me. Regarding relationships, I learned:

1. Don't let men talk to you crazy.
2. Leaving a heated situation and returning when you

felt like it is how to handle conflict. Storming out is even more impactful; the other person will obviously get your drift and they'll know better than to cross you the next time.

3. Strong women avoid drama like this. Unfortunately, being a strong woman didn't mean identifying, understanding, and relaying my feelings effectively. I am still learning how to do that.

When I think of families I saw beyond my own household, there were divorces, disrespect and disdain all over the place. There was emotional pain...trauma. Many studies have followed the lifelong impact childhood traumatic events have on one's quality of life. Adverse Childhood Experiences, or ACEs, is a research or screening tool that identifies childhood traumas and health statuses. Studies show that those who endured consistent, extreme stressors like abuse, neglect, and/or loss during formative years have an increased risk of experiencing mental and physical health issues later in life. This includes everything from major depression to hypertension. ACEs are also linked to negative emotions and behaviors that go unchecked.

There are also some cultural layers that the ACEs studies don't touch on that take us to a whole new ballpark. As a Black man, my dad is automatically a survivor of trauma. Stress, pain and loss, along with their problematic symptoms, were passed down. From slavery to sharecropping, through Jim Crow to police brutality and the ongoing the struggle for equality, there are both directly experienced traumas and vicarious traumas, meaning negative health symptoms related to simply hearing about these events.

The tough, distrustful, badass exterior I grew seeing didn't manifest overnight. Years of witnessing the things he encountered in his own FOO negatively altered his perception earlier than it should have. Survivors of trauma have few choices when faced with a real or perceived threat to their physical and emotional safety. They feel they will actually die when triggered to remember a hurtful event. In order to avoid this impending doom, they will fight: argue, push back, or literally throw jabs. They may activate the flight option: withdraw, become passive-aggressive, physically run away. There is also a freeze option, where the person doesn't know what to do!

Keeping fight or flight trauma responses in mind, I understand how Daddy's snide remarks were a way to withdraw from interacting with certain people. Perhaps he would say those things in order to discourage meaningful friendships (flight, as relationships can be a threat to one's security). His tendency to force his opinion on others, whether he knew it or not, was likely a way to defend against the threats to his own emotional safety. Or perhaps, his strategy was to appease the voices that tore him down to his deepest insecurity. There comes a point when, after enduring so much trauma, one's overall development becomes stunted. In my dad's case, his emotional maturity probably peaked mid-adolescence. This was clear in the ways he responded to verbal disagreement.

His grind ethic was developed out of a desire to better his circumstances, yet he still found ways to tear others down, including his own family. There is potential for a guy like him because I think he has a genuine desire to be healthy, although so far, it's only on his terms. A positive change would mean a certain level of vulnerability that he may not be ready for. Unfortunately, the generational cycles he ran from are ones he was doomed to repeat in his own family.

There is a vicious merry-go-round we all see in our families: traumatic event>emotional and physical response>neglect of said emotions>repeat. It's a wonder there are well-adjusted people in this world, right? Truth is, the healthiest of us likely came from difficult backgrounds. It makes all the difference if we can acknowledge there is something more for us than where we came from. We can break the chains of generational patterns in our families. Step One is freeing ourselves from denial.

I MENTIONED EARLIER that clients get an almost ominous vibe when I bring up Daddy Issues. Why is it so terrible to mention? We have society to thank for that. First of all, there is a gender stereotype that is all wrong. Countless articles, ads, shows, etc. that paint the picture of a woman with DI as a love-struck, clingy woman who only dates older men. You probably already know, the images aint pretty. Allow me to break down a few of the archetypes of women with DI and how they are presented in the media.

THE DADDY'S Girl

I talk a lot about spectrums when I'm facilitating therapy. Despite what people believe, there are times when it is ok to live in the gray area. For instance, if I forget to give my kids something green on their plates and automatically shout "I'm a bad mom!" to myself, that's clearly not fair. I'd be living in a black-and-white world where it's either "good moms" or "bad moms." Truth be told, remembering to make broccoli for dinner doesn't make me the best mother either. I have to think of the good things in between (the gray area) and accept that I'll have my good days and not-so-good days. And even on the not-so-good days, I can still find a silver lining.

FOR WOMEN who have great relationships with their fathers, it may be harder to see where you have DI. My best friend asked me, in the most loving way, how she would be able to relate to this material when she has a good relationship with her dad (he's amazing, by the way). It's a valid question. Consider who raised you. Our interactions with other people are informed by what we learned in the households we grew up in. Women in this category are portrayed as the apples of their fathers' eyes. They are typically doted upon and don't want for much.

FOR EXAMPLE, let's take Yara Shahidi's character, Zoe, on FreeForm's TV series *Grownish*. She was raised in a two-parent household; her mother is a doctor and father a successful executive at a marketing firm. Before leaving for college, she lived in a beautiful home in the suburbs of Los Angeles and went to a private school. Her parents supported her financially and trusted her decisions as a young adult. Zoe was what some would call spoiled rotten, as demonstrated by her access to pretty much anything she wanted and more. Her father would often have heart-to-heart talks with her. He listened to her needs and validated her, for the most part.

· · ·

ONE EPISODE, Zoe's actions caught up with her. She was off atschool abusing adderall and partying instead of hitting the books. One night when she stayed out so late, she didn't study for a final and felt the need to cheat her way through the exam. Well, the poor child got caught and when her father found out, Zoe was cut off. It was a lesson she was bound to learn: Take more responsibility and find your own way. Like most men who idolize their daughters the way hers did, it was likely even harder for him to teach. Imagine the questions he had to ask himself. He may have considered where he went wrong. The "shoulda-coulda-wouldas" were probably ringing loud in his head. Self-blame is an emotion many parents feel in situations where they find their kids doing wrong.

THE **DADDY'S Girl** is usually supported fully and adequately taken care of, even if her parents aren't working white collar jobs. She can call on her father for what she needs and like the doting dad, he will come to the rescue. Loving and supporting a little girl is not a cardinal sin. In fact, it's great! Here, the DG has a chance to learn how "a princess should be treated" and that "the world is hers."

A CHILD CAN NEVER HAVE TOO much support. But, don't forget the spectrum, where balance is necessary. When do caregivers take off the training wheels to teach life skills? Like many parenting mistakes, this style can affect a woman's ability to accept anything less than a "yes." She may expect to be pleased in any way, by any means necessary. Yes, this girl may also be the brat. On the flip side, though, this girl can be the most humble, appreciative person you'd meet.

. . .

I HAD a client who had been a caregiver for her father most of her life. Due to his illness, she had Power of Attorney over his finances. Since age 8, she'd cooked, cleaned, and cared for her father. She anticipated his every need appropriately and was praised for it. "He always told me how appreciative he was when I thought to clean the kitchen, so he wouldn't have to," she said.

She received a healthy amount of admiration and support from her sick father, and yet, still developed low self-esteem. In session, she shared that when she went to college and didn't get the same praise, she questioned whether her work was good enough. She was unable to stand her ground in conflict, and therefore was only recently finding her voice as an adult. In new relationships, she wondered if she had done something wrong if she didn't anticipate the needs of her partner. Although I am 99% sure her father didn't mean to contribute to this narrative, there was still an impact on her ability to confidently handle business and personal situations.

THERE ARE several archetypes between the two extremes of the bratty DG and the humble DG. We have to be aware of many other factors that play a role. We would do well to go back to the root of the irrational narrative.

THE APPROVAL SEEKERS

Have you ever been in the classroom with a little girl they call the "teacher's pet"? Me too. It's so annoying. As time goes on, this person evolves into that one who always asks questions at a conference...right before lunch time. It looks different in various settings, but the theme is usually one who wants to have the attention of the presenter or the room. This person is likely dealing with a "people pleasing" mentality that is steeped in low self-esteem issues. It's nice to be validated by others. Positive reinforcement goes a long way, especially if it was missing in their FOO or home.

MY CLIENT, let's call her Sally, knows the pain and exhaustion of this behavior all too well. She presented to therapy with symptoms of Generalized Anxiety Disorder, where she was constantly worrying about several things at one time. She lost sleep over what she should have said or done in certain exchanges at work and in personal relationships. When we did some deep diving into her one of her core beliefs, "I'm not good enough," we found she learned this early from her father. He was a busy man. So busy that he would work through important events Sally and her siblings had after school. When he did come up for air, it was to criticize and voice that if she was going to "waste his time" with a presentation, it needed to be better.

THERE WAS one particular memory she had of polishing a dance routine to perform at the football game, just for him-- but he didn't show. Sally strived in just about everything she did from then on. She wanted to impress the father who wasn't paying attention. After a while, she gave up seeking his approval and settled for that of anyone who paid any attention: teachers, friends, intimate partners, colleagues. She began to thrive from the praise she got, something she had been seeking since she was a child. We processed through instances where she felt at the top of her game, because she had developed such a great work ethic. The funny thing about appearances, though, is that things aren't always what they seem.

BEHIND CLOSED DOORS, Sally was rattled by days she'd just survived, having performed 16 hours for everyone else but exhausted by the mask she was wearing. She confirmed her mission was to gain approval from others in her professional life. She had also donned the mask for intimate relationships in an effort to hide the brokenness she felt. At the core, she wanted her father to hear of all the great things she was building in her life on personal and professional levels. She ended up learning there was a certain level of acknowledgement and understanding she needed to come to grips with on her own.

THE GOLD DIGGERS

Sugar Daddies. Yup. That's still a Thing. There are countless live websites catered to young women who are seeking older men to provide financial assets for them. The trips. The designer clothes. The lavishly decorated homes. The padded bank accounts. This is probably one of the most common stereotypes pumped out by the media regarding a woman with Daddy Issues. We are to assume that these women are simply in it for the money. That they have superficial motives.

· · ·

"DESTINY" came to counseling because her doctor recommended she find out the root cause of her needing treatment several times for sexually transmitted diseases. Though initially skeptical, eventually she started telling me about her situationship with a man who was taking care of her and her kids. He wasn't the first man to shower her with gifts. She usually dated guys who would buy her nice gifts during the course of their relationship. She learned early the cost of what she believed to be the star treatment: Eventually, they abandoned her after sex. She held onto hope that she would one day meet Prince Charming. She really thought it would pan out this time because he had been pretty consistent in taking her out to eat and at least asking about her children.

HER STORY REVEALED the absence of a father and a mother who worked long hours. She was raised mostly by her grandparents who were tired of rearing children; they only took her in to keep her out of the foster system. Destiny wasn't taught life skills that allowed her to thrive. But she did learn that keeping a man around meant food on the table and clothes on her back, as long as she kept them entertained.

NATURALLY, her go-to method for entering a relationship was based on survival. She thought she needed a man who would take care of her. She knew she was barely wanted in her family at this point and didn't have the confidence to learn how to make it on her own. It's an age-old cycle of taking the easy way out. The high-profile man she would search for was a means to an end. She was able to finally tell me she wasn't enjoying what she did. It was just the simplest way to feed herself and her two children.

THE STORY OF THE "GOLD DIGGER" is steeped in self-doubt, low self-worth, and many times trauma. I also want to point out the intersectionality that comes with the territory of categorizing women with DI. The GD could just as easily be the woman who was raised with a doting father. She could expect that any man she meets needs to achieve the high standards her father set for her. It looks like anything from dating the drug dealer who makes mad paper to seeking the stable man with status: doctors, lawyers, etc. We can't be fooled by the origin behind this mentality.

THE CLINGY TYPE

"I can't figure out why I keep calling my ex-boyfriend 100 times," Mary said to me during her intake. She was a 20-something woman who came to me because she was losing sleep thinking of the relationship she'd lost two weeks prior. "He just keeps ignoring me. I feel rejected and for some reason, this is how most of my breakups go down."

MARY REPORTED sexual assault in her past from the stepfather who raised her. She knew her biological father to be a career criminal; he was "too busy being in and out of jail over my life," Mary told me. When I asked how she typically reacted during relationships, she told me she constantly checked Instagram and Snapchat to peep out her lover's location.

. . .

MORE WORK REVEALED she had issues with trust and was deathly afraid of being hurt. She was tired of feeling on edge; the anxiety was overwhelming. Mary learned early what she didn't want in a relationship: the discomfort of being left over and over by someone who was supposed to protect her. "I guess, when I found someone who was interested, I hung on. I didn't want to be alone," Mary said in a light-bulb moment. We processed how hard it can be to let something go when you finally feel alive.

RELATIONSHIPS DO that for us sometimes. Mary's sexual assault experience made her feel numb. She said she never knew she could do more than exist until she started dating someone who touched her only when she consented. She walked me through the heartbreak of losing the first relationship that brought her back to life, and how she didn't have the skills to let go because she thought it was her only shot at happiness. Her belief that she would be alone only got stronger when she kept losing relationships with these men after her anxiety presented as clinginess.

MARY QUESTIONED her self-worth the entire time. If her boyfriend was three minutes late, or didn't text back right away, her mind was off to the races. She described what she called "desperate attempts" to gain attention she actually would have been able to keep without the anxious behavior.

. . .

MARY ALSO DESCRIBED how her symptoms manifested into the "jealous friend" type. It took her time to adjust to making friends in the first place. One major stuck point, a rule or negative belief that drives actions for a survivor of trauma, is that she can't trust people. She decided the best way to protect herself from embarrassment, awkward encounters and pain was to avoid engaging. Much like the boys she dated, she found that connecting with other people as friends was decent and wanted to hang on to the feeling. Her inability to manage her insecurities during these relationships made it difficult for her to have healthy friendships where she didn't feel the need to perform to hang on.

THE PROMISCUOUS TYPE

This is another age-old tale: woman meets someone. She and her partner court for a while--or maybe she doesn't--and they have sex. She may even do it before getting married...gasp! Then, after a while, she may get tired of that partner and it's on to the next. She isn't emotionally invested, may have gotten pregnant a couple times. She may have had the kids, maybe not. And, big shocker, she may also be labeled as a Gold Digger. We hear several, terrible ways to describe behavior that may feel natural to women, especially. No matter how much of an ally we are to "these women," we fall into negative judgment that perpetuates an unsafe environment for healing and acceptance for the PT.

MY GENERATION TRIED to reclaim all sexual derogatory terms via a movement Amber Rose championed, where she took pride in her sexual freedom and demanded she and her fellow, liberated women not be "slut shamed." I have been in rooms with women my age and older who ask where this woman's father is, which is a valid question. But we often fail to ask the more important questions.

THERE ARE SEVERAL LAYERS HERE. Firstly, the negative perception usually speaks more about the person demonizing the sexually free woman than it does about the woman herself. We have to consider one's values about what sex is and even define promiscuity in the first place. As a therapist, I usually approach from a trauma-informed lens. I assess, wondering if there is any history of childhood sexual abuse and, if so, how long she endured this pain. I probe for how she developed her perception of sex and how she uses it, what it means to her, etc.

BUT SEXUAL TRAUMA isn't part of everyone's story. Sex serves a purpose. You define it how you want: Stress reliever, entertainment, connection with a partner, appreciation for taking out the trash, the means to pay bills, etc. Sexual expression is just that: an expression of one's voice. There is something about having choices in this arena that is empowering. Feeling seen adds to our value, whether we want to admit it or not. Sex is one way to do it.

I STRONGLY BELIEVE things don't just come out of nowhere. So, during an initial intake with a patient, I'll explore where their messages come from. There are certain messages, about sex especially, that stick to them. As they pour out regrets and shame about the subject, they're not only talking about the stigma associated with media stereotypes. There are scripts, if you will, that they've lived by since childhood. I often ask: Was there conversation about sex with your parents at all? I'm talking more than the Birds-N-Bees talk. How did you learn about it? What did your mother say? How did your father influence your views about sex?

THE LATTER CAN BE a tough question, because some women must come to grips about how impactful absence truly is. Perhaps the father was not physically present at all. Or the absence of the conversation about sex hits hard. They wonder, "What if my dad actually taught me about boys, sex, relationships?" They realize the impact of being left to their own devices to figure it out. Yeah, there are women who tell me they use sex as a currency and are looking for love in the wrong places. There are some who use sex to rebel against their fathers, sneaking boys in their rooms since adolescence. Most admit having their fathers present (physically, emotionally, and otherwise) could have made a positive influence. Either way, "promiscuity" looks like many things. I found it to be more than "being fast." This language in itself perpetuates a narrative we need to change.

WOMAN on the Defense

Kelly Clarkson wrote a beautiful ballad called "Because of You" that expresses how she was impacted by her own DI. She sings, "Because of you, I never stray too far from the sidewalk," which is a powerful statement about the fear she learned growing up in the home she did. She goes on to tell us how difficult it was to cry because her father perpetuated the myth that this is a sign of weakness. She knew not to get too close to anyone, as a way to protect her heart. I'm sure the final blow was the divorce of her parents, when there were inevitable adjustments she had to make to life as she knew it.

I SIT with many women who have that same guard up. After years of dealing with heartbreak by a man who was there, but left, was emotionally unavailable, dictated instead of listened and supported, etc., options are slim. As far as they're concerned, it's time to put up the wall, wear the mask, and avoid pain at all costs. This woman may appear standoffish in a social function, with her guard up looking for the next person to hurt her. She may be disinterested in the relationship she is in, if she pursues one at all. She may be the mother who is triggered by her own children, so that her anxiety looks like anger when her security is threatened by the random things kids do. There is grace to give; she may be uptight, but it's for good reason.

"IT'S SCARY TO LET GO," said a Jessica, 24-year-old client. "If I let someone in, they may hurt me like my dad. They may want something from me I can't give, then I look crazy." Jessica watched her once-revered father cheat on her mother and was placed in the middle of the drama. As a 9-year-old experiencing overwhelming emotions that she didn't have the language for at the time, she was incapable of answering questions about her parents' relationship. She just knew it didn't feel right. Her parents divorced, and when her father took her for custodial visits, he spent much of the time trying to win her allegiance and respect. After a while he just gave up, the nail in the coffin for a girl with DI.

SINCE THEN, she understood her problem to be centered around broken trust. She learned to question the motives of others and of herself. This narrative drove her friendships, career decisions, even her choice of vehicle. It eventually spiraled into anxiety that was severe enough to interfere with her ability to build meaningful relationships. When she came to counseling, she said she didn't do much for fun, unless you count staying home and watching Netflix alone. "I just keep popping off; I don't do people," she said.

THE TRUTH IS, there are many different ways DI can manifest. They're unique and go across the board because, wait for it...we ALL have DI. African-American, West Indian, male, female; it affects us all. We have been raised by people who have their own issues with their fathers too. No wonder! This seeps into the family unit in the sneakiest of ways. There's only so much time these symptoms can fly under the radar before we realize there's a problem. I have a story that will demonstrate my own revelation.

I WAS 19 years old and in love after a few months of getting to know my boyfriend, now husband, Tony. By then I had two years of college under my belt and was slated to move into my first off-campus apartment with my best friend. I was definitely an adult. It was our first summer together, and Tony and I planned a beach trip.

· · ·

THIS WAS A BIG DEAL. I was going to spend two whole nights in a new city with the man I adored. I was on my grown woman shit. I had gotten everything done on the checklist: booked the hotel, took off work, budgeted for souvenirs, and packed cute outfits. The last thing on the list was to check in with my parents. I considered myself to be a respectful and responsible person. So, I called Mommy to tell her where I was going and with whom.

"OK, Baby. Have fun and be safe," she said. That was easy. She had already met Tony and really liked him. She knew how much he cared for me and he was already becoming part of the family. She called him her son-in-law from the start. Thankfully, that didn't scare him off!

DADDY WAS GOING to be a harder sell. Although he had not lived in the family house for over a decade and I had been away at college most of the year, I still felt the need to inform him. At that point, our relationship was a bit rocky. He had moved on past my mother with another woman, who was living with him and discussing marriage, which was a sore subject between us. On top of that, he had already bailed on several meetings I had set up for him to meet Tony.

ON AT LEAST THREE OCCASIONS, I had arranged everyone's schedules to introduce the two of them. This wasn't easy, as I was in college and living an hour away. But, I was the respectful daughter trying to do the right thing. Or was I still acting out of fear because I was conditioned to look for a negative consequence if I went against his word? I knew the rules. I was positive my dad wanted to lay eyes on the man his daughter was dating. So I tried to arrange a meet-n-greet way before the beach trip. When my attempts didn't pan out, I didn't hesitate to tell Daddy about my disappointment.

"DADDY, you were supposed to meet us at Applebees an hour ago," I told him after about 20 minutes of waiting with Tony. My dad was always on time, early even. So I knew after 5 minutes he wasn't coming. But I held on to hope. It was embarrassing and disappointing.

"When did I tell you that? I never said I was coming, Christian. You know I have to write." There was always a deadline for so many projects. He was a very important person, and he never let me forget that.

"Ok, then," I said, hoping he would hear the disappointment in my voice and tell me he was hopping in the car.

"I'll holler at you later. We can do this another time," he said. Before ending the call, he made a half-assed effort to reschedule.

THIS WAS another instance when I felt disregarded. I was doing my best to navigate a relationship with him as an adult, but felt like I was failing. Although we hardly spoke about anything meaningful during my adolescence, he expected me to follow a code: I was the child and he was the adult. But I got fed up and began trying new things to be heard. Using my voice was taking some getting used to for both of us. Needless to say, this beach trip was coming at a fragile time in our relationship. My efforts were ignored, yet, I was faulted for not introducing him to my boyfriend.

I CONTACTED my dad when everything was booked for the trip to tell him that I was going away with a man he hadn't met. I decided to tell him in a public place to minimize the potential catastrophe. After my shift at Old Navy ended, we met in the food court of Columbia Place Mall.

"SO, um, I'm going to Myrtle Beach with my boyfriend," I stammered. I was visibly nervous. My voice shook; I could barely maintain eye contact. It was a little harder to have this conversation in person than I'd imagined. I continued, "I figured I would leave the car with Alex," so my brother could get to his job while I was gone. I had it all planned out.

"WHAT YOU MEAN GOING to the beach?" Daddy had a way of sending the most chilling sensation to my gut, literally just by speaking. "I haven't even met dis dude," he scoffed. He was clearly disgusted.

"WELL, I just thought it was taking so long for all of us to get together." I didn't reference the fact that he was the one holding everything up.

"SO, YOU WAIT," he retorted. "What your momma say about this?"

.   .   .

"SHE WAS FINE. She said 'Be careful and have fun.' She's met Tony already," I said with a glimmer of hope that the conversation would end here. The look on his face told me it wasn't. He had more to say and I knew where it was going.

"UGH, of course she did. You know, I'm going to talk to her," he said. "And how you gonna just leave your car with Alex? That's not yours anyway, I can take that whenever I need to."

IT WAS HEART WRENCHING. Yeah, the car was about 10 years old at the time, but she was mine. Cindy the Sentra had been his sister's car, which he arranged for me to have when she was ready to buy a new one.

"WHY WOULD YOU DO THAT? I'm coming right back to get it from Alex when I come home. How will I get to work?" I asserted myself. I was deliberate with my language so he heard that I was going on this trip--done deal. I wasn't backing down.

"YOU TRY IT, see if I don't take them keys," he said walking away from the table.

I TRIED to tell myself that my dad probably just wanted to protect me, but I was holding onto a fantasy that our relationship would manifest into that of me being a Daddy's Girl. I wanted to be doted on. I would have enjoyed him meeting the man who was dating me and giving him "the talk" in a loving, yet stern way. But he had had his chance--three times. I was hanging on to a dream that wouldn't come true. Instead of the caring dad who was watching his little girl grow up, I experienced the angry man grasping at straws to hold on to power long after he'd left.

I DON'T REMEMBER TALKING to Daddy much after he and I spoke in the food court. Part of me hoped he would forget the plans altogether. Nah. My phone rang with him on the other end the morning of the trip.

"WHAT YOU DOIN?" He asked. No, he didn't greet me with a hello, after days of not speaking.

"I'M PACKING to go to the beach," I said. Straight like that. I was sure he was just testing me. I'm even more positive he knew I was terrified.

"CHRISTIAN. If you try leaving this city, I'll be right over there to stop you," he told me.

THE PANIC SET IN. I was deathly afraid of what he might do to Tony. The poor guy already had enough to deal with; I had given him an ear-full about what went down in the food court the previous week. This couldn't be the first time they met! I quickly threw the last of my things into my bag. I was ready to leave the car key under the mat. If Daddy got there when Tony was pulling up there no telling what would go down.

"YOU DON'T NEED to do that! We already have everything booked, I saved all my money. Why are you trying to ruin this for me?" I was desperate. I hated that I sounded like I was begging, but this called for extreme measures.

"OH, you think you're grown, disrespecting me like that. I'm on my way, I don't want to hear---" click. I hung up and dialed Tony on the other line.

THOSE WHO KNOW me well can tell you my favorite Disney movie of all time: *The Little Mermaid*. I was 3 years old when the original animation came out. I can recite the script verbatim, hum the score from memory. It's forever ingrained in me. It wasn't until recently when I realized that besides great hair and cute singing voices, there was another connection I had with Ariel: we both have Daddy Issues. She wanted to be heard and find her own way, even if it meant going against her father, King Triton. When she saved Prince Eric that day on the beach, she was smitten. She dreamed of meeting him again and was determined to meet him (on the beach) again some day. Ariel was me. Prince Eric was Tony. We were fighting against all odds to be together, even if it meant challenging my father.

THERE WAS a scene in the movie when King Triton tells Ariel she will follow his way or else. When she tells him she is riding for her Prince, the King goes berserk and destroys her collection of human objects. It was his desperate act to assert his authority instead of embracing his daughter as she was coming into her own.

I TRIED my best to explain my feelings of impending doom to Tony. "Daddy! Mad! Coming! Hurry!" After what probably sounded like frantic gibberish, my knight in shining armor told me he was headed my way. Thankfully, he lived a few minutes down the road. We were on I-20 in record time. During the entire three-hour ride, I questioned if I was doing the right thing. I wondered what would happen when I got home and if I would actually get in trouble at 19 years old.

I REMEMBER one spanking when I was about 4. We were living in New Mexico. Mommy was leaving for her night job when Daddy returned from working on the base. She had just finished giving us our dessert, chocolate ice cream. I remember wanting more and decided I would ask for it after she left. This was my first memory of telling a lie. I told Daddy I hadn't gotten any dessert that night, and he obliged when I asked him for more ice cream. Welp. I was a few spoonfuls into my bowl of sweet, creamy goodness when Mommy walked back in the door; she had forgotten something. Imagine my surprise---and hers--- when she caught me mid-bite.

"WHY YOU LOOKING at her like that?" Daddy inquired.

. . .

"SHE JUST HAD ice cream before you got home," she snitched. I was mortified. I knew it was wrong when I told the fib. And I felt it. Remember that scene from *The Jacksons: An American Dream* where the young actor portraying the young Michael Jackson ran and hid from his dad to avoid a butt whipping? That was me, except I got caught. It was the first and last beating I remember receiving.

FAST FORWARD TO the 19-year-old me. Punishment. Surely, that doesn't happen to a grown person, right? After all, Daddy was far removed from my life in regards to parenting. I didn't even know what getting in trouble looked like anymore. I think the worst thing he could have done was take the car away like he promised to. It's amazing, frightening even, the hold he had on me even while he was slowly removing himself from my life.

I REMEMBER TRYING SO hard to remain poised; I didn't want Tony to think I was crazy. I was still trying to impress him after all. He had already watched me frantically navigate the situation. I started to feel better once we were a little closer to our destination. I managed to hold it together. Oh, but when we got to the hotel room, I cried. Like. A. Big. Baby. So much for our first getaway. Tony held me the whole time while I repeated "Daddy doesn't love me," over and over. It was a really sad scene. I'm sure I freaked him out. I was a mixture of emotions: Afraid of what I would go home to; anxious about my first overnight trip with a man; relieved that we made it safely. Disrespected, depressed, embarrassed, yet in love all the same. It was overwhelming.

. . .

WE WERE able to salvage the trip after that weekend, although I don't remember much of what we did. What I do remember is the anxiety. No, I didn't think Daddy would jump out of the ocean like King Triton and chase us away. But I could hear his critical tone from my childhood about making better choices. I questioned all my moves since being a little girl because I hadn't had the chance to exercise my own judgment. The choices I made were always based out of fear. I was nervous about the outcome because I had seen my dad's wrath.

HE DIDN'T PLAY when it came to discipline. I was serious when I said it only took me one time to lie to my dad. I didn't want to feel that kind of pain I saw him inflict on my brother, Alex. My dear brother. He presented a different challenge for my dad. I can remember several instances when he pushed boundaries. His shenanigans at school always beat us home, in the form of messages waiting on the answering machine for our parents to hear. Alex was punished for small things. I remember when he didn't want to change his handwriting to a larger font for his third grade teacher to read. After a conversation with him and the teacher wasn't enough, Daddy went to swinging. He used the hard, buckle end of the belt and whaled on my brother until he didn't have any screams left in him. Mommy and I cowered in the corner while he made a production of it all.

AS I THINK BACK on how the beach trip went down, I can't help but think of how the old me would invalidate my responses. It's a knee-jerk reaction that comes from the notion that my "feelings are not valid," something I didn't have the language for as a kid, but certainly felt. The old me would talk about how immature I was as a 19-year-old who was only acting out of her emotions. I can talk about what I should have done, etc. But the grown, 33-year-old me, the me who has been doing her work and is more confident and free, says forget all that!

WE'VE all done things we wish we could change; being out of sync and thinking with an underdeveloped brain is part of the process. It is when we decide to be more aware of the unhelpful thoughts and restructure our emotional responses that we come out on top. I mentioned feeling embarrassed, hurt, disregarded, anxious, etc. These are all emotions. They were coming from somewhere. A learned place. Recall the FOO. We follow the models within our families to make sense of things, all the way down to their thought processes. There is a strong difference between what we think and what we feel. Knowing the difference is the key to successfully taking back the power lost when we are dealing with symptoms of DI.

EVERY CLIENT that walks through my door is going to learn the A>B>C Model. I use it to teach them the relationship between the activating event (A), the belief (B), and the consequences (C), which are emotions and behaviors. When something happens, there is an activation of a belief system. For instance, when Daddy stood me up to meet Tony more than once (A), I thought, *I must not be important enough* (B), and therefore felt insecure (C). It gets even more overwhelming when we consider that we can think multiple things at once, which I refer to as a thought spiral: *He must not care about who I see; Why is his work more important than me? Does he just want to spend time with his new wife at home instead of the daughter who needs him?* All these thoughts led to feelings of anxiety, sadness, confusion, and disregard.

I'VE COME to realize there's power in recognizing my negative thought spirals. Calling them out takes away the intimidation of being under the weight of my own mind. If I can stop the spiral long enough to talk myself out of it (*Christian, you're not making sense. It's more to do with his own issues...stop making it yours. Enjoy your moment. Go for a walk*), then I'm in a better position to shift my emotions and improve my mood. This takes practice. When you get really good at admitting things to yourself, then you can tap into saying these things to trusted people. By then you will have started replacing these negative thoughts with positive things to talk yourself into feeling better. You can share them with others and relate to their struggles, taking some gems from what they've learned. Healing is completely possible as long as you remember you are not alone. When you have intentions of taking back your headspace, breaking the cycle of thoughts that keep you trapped, and remembering your are here for a purpose, you unlock knowledge and skills no one can take away from you.

"I WANT to help you expand your emotional vocabulary," I tell my clients. So, I equip them with another one of my favorite tools: The Feelings Wheel. You'll see a variation of this graphic below, where a few basic emotions are found: happy, surprised, bad, sad, disgusted, angry, and fearful.

These are called secondary emotions, meaning the feelings that present to everyone else. What we need to get in tune with and acknowledge are the primary emotions, which you will see further out along the wheel. For instance, we will likely feel disrespected, hurt, or embarrassed before we feel angry. Imagine how much we take, how much we tell ourselves before we are finally angry. This notion in itself demonstrates the way our thought patterns brew before we blow up!

I DON'T RECALL what happened when I finally returned home from the beach, probably because nothing did. It was so anticlimactic. In a strange way, I felt relieved to avoid more drama, yet I also felt insecure that Daddy didn't fight to mend things; he just gave up on me and decided to ostracize Tony in his own passive-aggressive way. So, I got to keep my car, which was nice. I returned to school and continued to travel up and down I-77 to visit Tony on the weekends.

LOOKING BACK on this situation through the lens of time shows me the energy I wasted on everything. This is another thing that helps when you're awakened to the power to change your thoughts/emotions: You remember where the worry took you last time and coach yourself through to avoid it. During the weeks that passed after the beach I began to realize my relationship with my dad wouldn't be what I'd imagined it could be. There was an obvious shift. I accepted there was no hope that our relationship would be the doting daddy and his prized princess. I wouldn't get the happy ending Ariel got when King Triton finally accepted her decision to be part of a world she'd dreamed of her whole life.

Our communication diminished, which may have been for the best, but I kept waiting for the other shoe to drop. I didn't realize it then, but I had a full-fledged case of DI. The way I kept replaying how I could change things about myself, what I'd done, how I could fix things. Man, the weight I felt under all that blame. The longer that went unchecked, the worse it got and transferred into other areas. It's kind of like a cold that can turn into pneumonia if we ignore the symptoms. Nevertheless, as long as we know the diagnosis, we can treat it properly.

IF YOU FALL into one of these categories of a woman with DI, if you're like me and there's an overlap and/or traits not even in this chapter, fear not! There's nothing wrong with you, sis. Things have happened to you. But the very acknowledgement of having DI is a major first step toward freedom. I've been dealing with the worst part of my DI symptoms for 15 years. Now as a woman in my early 30s, I've defeated things I didn't have the gall to tackle before. I overcame my fears, stamped out the shame, and remembered I was born with power.

WHAT TO DO next

Many wonder, *why bring up these feelings at all?* Especially if they have already packed away the pain, thinking it will never resurface. "It's only going to ruin my life and I'm past that," they say to me. Well, we have to uproot the ugly to know what lies beneath. We can't address something that we choose not to see. When cleaning house, we sweep up all the dirt, then we dump it. This is the same concept with facing the crap. So we have to identify the triggers, people/places/things that cause a negative thought spiral.

BUT WE DON'T STOP THERE. Part of this process of healing is taking care of yourself also. Recall the template for self-care in the beginning. I cannot stress this enough: take care of your mental, physical, spiritual, and emotional body. Truth is, we don't know where or who this discovery may lead us to. It may be a dark place. That said, make sure you have a healthy set of coping skills ready to use when the work gets to be too much. I'm hoping for positive change, but it may take a while to get there. Just think community. Community is what I hope you find here, in my story.

COLLECTIVE Unconscious

You're not alone! There are many women with the same realizations I had. One thing I learned from author and researcher Brene Brown, who has spent over two decades studying courage, vulnerability, shame, and empathy, is that shame cannot live in community. The feeling of connection, that #metoo mentality is the perfect ground for positive change.

AN EARLY PSYCHOTHERAPIST, Carl Jung, tells us that we all have a tacit connection to one another. It's in the form of memories, experiences, a common thread of some sort. Ever meet someone who seemed so in tune with you because you went through similar things? You may have built a lifelong friendship based on that instant rapport.

. . .

DI IS treatable because of things like the collective unconscious. The connectedness we experience stamps out the shame. Remember, those negative thought spirals can't live in empathy and relatability. It's like an antidote. By tapping into what we already have inside us and sharing with one another, we begin the healing.

SIX

Self-Care Check-in

1. How has your FOO impacted you? How has your perception of yourself, others, and things around you been shaped?
2. Was your father in the picture? How did his presence influence your worldview? What are the good and not-so-good parts of his influence in your early life?
3. Was your father not in the picture? What are your thoughts and feelings about his absence?

This intro has potential to trigger certain feelings. Do you know what they are? Let's lean in to how complex our emotions are. Check out the feelings wheel illustration below. You will notice the basic or secondary emotions are found in the middle. The further you go out along the pie, the more intense the emotions are. Why does this matter? Because knowing exactly how you feel will point to your need. For example, if you feel disrespected by someone, you may consider setting a boundary to protect your peace. If you are feeling let down, you may be OK with your favorite pint of ice cream! Either way, sit with the emotion, sis. Try to tune in to what they are telling you.

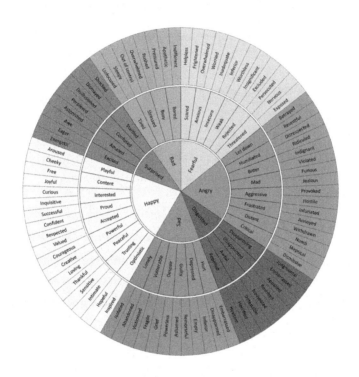

ACTIVITY:

If you located the emotion(s) brought up by this chapter, notice where it manifests in your body. For example, fear (AKA anxiety) shows up in the pit of my gut along with a wave of heat down my spine. This tells me I need something cool to drink to get to a decent enough headspace to really assess and meet my needs.

Use this information throughout the book. Build on the skill set you are refining: self-awareness.

SEVEN

Attachment Styles

"Therapy is like parenting your inner child." I heard that on a podcast once, and have repeated it to many of my own clients. It's such a true and powerful statement. Whether you refer to this process as your "journey," "walk," "self-exploration," "path" or actual therapy, the work will always require a look at what your younger self needed to feel safe and secure. This is what makes for a difficult, but effective experience. By now, you know how crucial it is to explore these roots during this process.

What truly makes someone tick? One of the oldest and most reliable theories in therapy is the nature versus nurture argument. We were created with a certain biological makeup; this is nature. Our personalities, characteristics, beliefs, and more are related to how we are nurtured. For example, might someone with a physical disability develop a negative mindset by focusing on their limitations? Or might their limitations foster a negative pattern of thoughts, words and actions? There's a chicken or the egg conundrum here.

If we dive a little deeper, we find conversations around the nurture aspect help us truly tap into the secret sauce to our essence. The way we are cared for by our village teaches us so much about our worldview. Our reactions are shaped by what we were taught (FOO) when dealing with triggers. The things that activate our beliefs/thought spirals (whether they are good or not so good) are different based on our unique experiences from the time we enter the world. For example, if we have a more positive outlook on things, we tend to roll with the punches. We subscribe to the notion that everything will work out. We can honestly accept that no matter what, nothing happens without helping us evolve into our best selves.

Even trust is learned from birth. Yes, birth! We learn who's worth our time based on whether your infant self was consistently cared for. After a while, you begin to understand who to go to when you need something and who to stay away from. Trust is built on being able to rely on someone, even if it is based on whether you got your bottle on time and a diaper change when you needed it. Sooner or later, we attach to those people who help us meet our basic needs. Imagine how different attachment would be for someone without a village, where it's different getting fed, clothed, and cared for.

What about women who have had a hard time engaging in a loving, trusting relationship with their fathers? I've had women tell me how they always knew better than to trust men because their dad wasn't there to begin with. This is where they learned to keep their defenses up, which impacted their relationships later on. Sooner or later they apply this same "you can't trust anyone" theory across other areas of their life: school, work, friendships...their own children.

On a different part of the spectrum, some women were given the opportunity to practice engaging in a healthy relationship with a father figure. Maybe their mom remarried a wonderful man or they had an adequate father figure step in. The child may have been past the "learning to trust" stage of life, but the learning curve can be less strenuous with proper support and a loving example of how to engage in a relationship like this. This gives us hope that positive change can happen!

Regardless, developing a healthy relationship as intimate as a Daddy-Daughter interaction takes engagement, especially if it's a totally new idea to someone that being securely attached is necessary to navigate life. This, my friend, is how we start breaking the stigma about DI: we start considering what impedes secure attachments for Daddy's Girls, who have been labeled Approval Seeking, Gold Digging, Clingy, Promiscuous, Women on the Defense. We empathize and support each other.

Attachment Theory

John Bowlby (1907-1990) was a British psychoanalyst and psychologist. He left a legacy that helps us understand the various levels of attachment between a child and their caregiver and its impact across the lifespan. This concept gives us perspective on what constitutes healthy mental and developmental functioning during varying life stages. Bowlby's main goal was to find out what gets in the way of the "lasting psychological connectedness between human beings." [cite: https://www.verywellmind.com/john-bowlby-biography-1907-1990-2795514]

His early studies involved watching the reactions of infants when their caregiver left the exam room. He noted the way the babies screamed bloody murder or appeared relatively calm. Some babies looked alright at first before they started to panic. After observing patterns and gathering data from feedback of the caregivers outside the exam room, Bowlby concluded that an adequate bond between a child and their caregiver is crucial for survival. A child's reaction to distress when their needs are not met says a lot about how much they trusted those who were in their corner. There are varying levels to attachment and they are related to survival rates.

When we consider the structure of one's FOO and the DI symptoms that manifest, we have to think about the strength of the bond a child has to their father. During the pre-attachment stage, the child doesn't quite know their caregivers, but are beginning to develop the level of trust necessary for survival. By seven months old, a child begins to recognize their village. They even have a preference for certain caregivers; if they don't recognize the person who cares for them, extreme levels of anxiety ensue [cite: https://www.simplypsychology.org/attachment.html]. This is also the same age infants develop a fear of strangers. In some cases, that can be the absentee parent.

We already established that an absent father is not restricted to physical absence. I submit that emotional absence can make someone look physically different. How does this impact a child who is trying to make sense of the world? Think of the confusion, anxiety, insecurity, and downright fear for their safety this breeds in a kid. Think of how this impacts their perception of every person who comes into their life, where they learned to test the validity of the connection since infancy. Consider how this changes the way a woman interacts with men after subscribing to the notion that ALL men are jerks and will cause pain because her father did.

Certain psychosocial behaviors depend on the level of attachment a person has. Meaning, the way we develop our sense of self, self worth and our view of others are based on what we learned during the crucial, formative years where attachments developed...or didn't. This spectrum ranges from secure to extremely anxious. We apply Bowlby's theory when discussing intimate relationships, friendships, partnerships, business deals, you name it. Interactions with others are extremely revealing of our strengths and limitations in this arena. Let's take a look at how attachment styles look in relationships.

Secure

This is where it's at, ladies. It's the bar Bowlby set for us to strive to. When this woman is in a relationship, she presents as a confident, trustworthy person who doesn't mind getting to know someone on a more personal level. In fact, she finds value in developing meaningful relationships. She has no fear when there is an opportunity to get close to someone because she knows she brings something to the table. When arguments arise she has no problem communicating her needs, whether in dating relationships, friendships or at work. She knows who she is and doesn't let anyone shake her sense of self.

Her childhood was most likely one where she was cared for in the most loving way. Her father may have been there, cheering her on. Maybe she had two mothers and no father at all. Whomever was in her village did a great job affirming her. Having an encouraging teacher, coach, cousin may have made all the difference in her firmly grounded sense of self.

She has no problem rolling with her own evolution in different life seasons.

I know a woman like this, who goes to my church. I consider Jessica a mentor because of what I have gleaned from her over the years. She is extremely grounded. I remember going to her whenever I felt like I was at a low point a few years back. I struggled with finances for a while and Jessica was there to offer advice.

"Girl, it took me a minute, too. I'm no expert, but check out this Suze Orman book," she told me. She was even confident in making this referral because she understood she didn't know it all--and that was fine.

"I just don't know how I'm supposed to make this all work. I have a son now, Tony hasn't proposed yet. I think I'm doing it all wrong," I would cry to her.

"Christian, the awesome part about this day is that God walked it before you, so you can't screw this up," Jessica said, smiling. She stressed to me that I wasn't the failure I thought I was, that I simply needed to do better, which was possible. I needed that gem to help me stop internalizing negativity.

Jessica was so candid with me. Her struggles were relatable. I understood I wasn't alone. She experienced her share of jerks, but told me she was able to come out on top most of the time because she knew she was loved by the people who mattered to her. Her dad was in her life. He encouraged her to go for her dreams, even when he thought it may be hard. Jessica said her father coached her on how to handle the curve balls life threw and let her know he would be there. She is what we call a Daddy's Girl. As it turned out, she had her share of issues with him. Shocker.

We have already established everyone has DI. Jessica was able to come into her own because she had a solid foundation that included her father from the beginning. She was securely attached spiritually, emotionally, and he was physically there. This made it possible for her to thrive sooner rather than later in life. But she also talked to me about the amount of pressure she fell under as she strove to impress her dad.

This is pretty typical, that we want to make our parents proud, but this attitude later manifested in pressure to anticipate the needs of the men she dated before she got married. It wasn't until she had kids of her own that she realized she had stretched herself so thin, she always considered herself last. Yeah, she was confident and she was poised. She could do anything anyone asked her to. She still can. Now, she can do these things with a different mindset, one that includes self-care and intentions of performing to what God called her to do rather than to someone else's expectations.

Let's check out these attachment styles.

Anxious

"Where. Is. My Riiiinngggg?!" I would yell at Tony when he pissed me off.

As much as I loved him from the beginning, I was so insecure in our relationship. I wanted to be married so badly after having his son and living together for about 6 months. My dad told me explicitly that Tony would leave me. It's a message that stuck with me until we were about 6 years into our relationship--it scared the shit out of me. After making it as far as sharing a lease with a man whose child we shared, I was sure I was on the way to breaking whatever curse my dad tried to speak over me. It just wasn't happening fast enough, for a number of reasons. One of them was surely the fact that I had not yet started repairing the damage from my DI. So, I nagged. I stomped my feet. I did everything short of making a powerpoint presentation on all the reasons we should be married.

Everything I did had to be perfect. I worked hard to make sure we had fun dates. We liked to travel, which meant I had to look good on my man's arm; shopping was out of control. I equated my worth with the way I looked. No matter how often Tony told me how fine I was, I didn't believe it. I was determined to make sure he didn't have any reason to leave me. I so wanted to prove my dad wrong.

Obviously, my motivation was all jacked up. Although I loved Tony, my disappointment in my dad's lack of support took precedence for a while. I was torn between my preoccupation with showing my dad we were still together and making Tony happy. All the while, I was clingy, needy, and downright afraid of what could happen if this relationship didn't work. Acting out of fear is obviously not healthy. It's where the most irrational thoughts and actions come from. If I didn't get the attention I needed I would go find it elsewhere. Sometimes, that was another man who told me I was pretty. It was excessive drinking at one point. The anxiety I lived with in our relationship in its younger years was so insistent. The thought spirals I got caught up in were relentless: *You're not doing this right; if Tony sees this, he'll leave you. You should have answered the phone on the first ring. What kind of meal was that? IF you even get a proposal, the marriage won't work; you are a terrible cook.* I still sometimes struggle with that latter thought, and remind myself that I may not be the best cook, but my marriage is still strong.

I didn't know at the time, but the way I interacted while dating was a direct reflection of my relationship with my dad as a kid. This anxious attachment style where I lived for words of affirmation and reassurance from external sources was a learned behavior. As a kid, I had Daddy in the house, yet still felt distant. It became worse when he and my mom separated. My intuition told me I needed to do something to keep his attention or lose him forever. My stellar grades, band performances, and chores around the house even after he moved out were all pleas for support from my dad. Thank God for growth. Thank God for the realization that this was in fact a problem and one can't sustain life on other people's approval alone.

Avoidant-Dismissive

A woman with this attachment style likely has a spotty past with her father or father figure. It's hard to be in a situation where the father comes around when he feels like it. Sometimes he's available for extracurriculars, sometimes he isn't. Maybe there was a misunderstanding with the other parent and it impacted his presence. What's for sure is the woman who dealt with the rollercoaster of emotions that accompanies a wishy-washy father, experiencing the unfulfilled hope and waves of disappointment, keeps her guard up.

This woman knows she wants a relationship, but doesn't trust her partner. She knows the value of connection theoretically, but also knows by experience how awful it can be. She will likely downplay the importance of intimacy as a way to get ahead of the pain she knows is coming. She will probably prefer a healthy distance from her partner; perhaps they live in different cities. It could mean she is not rushing to move in with her partner, in fact she is totally fine with going days without speaking to her partner.

Carrie came to me a few years ago because she was annoyed with her girlfriend, Jasmine. Like most people complaining about their partners, the problem wasn't her.

"She always wants me to check in. I'm at the studio," Carrie told me. "I don't have time to let her know all my moves."

While I understood the potential damage of clinginess, I couldn't help but wonder what Carrie's relationship scripts were. That is, I had to know the messages she took away from watching her folks as she grew up.

"What should a relationship look like," I asked.

"I do me, she does her. When I feel like I'm ready to talk, I call her," Carrie said confidently. She was definitely a woman who knew what she wanted.

We processed her ideals a little more, discussing where she learned the dynamics of a relationship. Amongst a heap of issues, we found that she indeed had moderate symptoms of DI. She told me she had to have the majority of control, but not for the reasons her girlfriend thought. Carrie, like many other women, was trying to protect herself from being hurt. That's what anxiety drives in us: the need to control any variable that may contribute to pain. Which makes sense. There is a function in our brain that identifies a threat and says "Shut down, fight, or run." Period. This shows up in relationships, where we are most vulnerable.

Intimacy is where we find ourselves exposed to things we may not have anticipated. It's where we learn how to navigate the nuances in communication, self-worth, etc.

Carrie eventually learned some of her unhealthy habits, such as closing herself off, appearing dismissive and being disconnected, were contributing to the demise of a relationship she actually valued. It was a big deal to admit that she indeed loved the woman she was with. She first had to face the impact of her father's reaction to who she loved. Carrie modeled a level of disapproval in her own relationships she didn't know came from her father's prejudice against lesbians. Now, this is not the story of everyone in the LGBTQIA2+ community. But it's important to acknowledge the distance created between her and her father, regardless of the reason.

She learned that revealing certain parts of herself would likely be met with disapproval. We know certain things logically, but it is different when they actually happen. Carrie knew she didn't want to feel that rejection again, and from then on she was on high alert.

Avoidant-Fearful

On the more extreme part of the spectrum was Sarah, a 35-year-old woman who couldn't fathom why relationships don't work out for her. She, too, understood the need for connection, but would only participate on her own terms.

"I can't seem to click with anyone," Sarah cried. She said in her dating life she had no barriers around sex or gender, but was more into vibing with the energy of another human being.

We explored the way her anxiety manifested, which was more fear-based than a genuine, rational concern. Sarah's father used to abuse her mother. Aside from learning how she didn't want to be treated by a man, she decided that while she admired her mother's strength in fighting back, she knew she wasn't totally invested in the idea of a relationship. Sarah found that she couldn't help the almost magnetic connection she had for certain people, but after practicing a lifestyle where she abstained from intimacy of all kinds, it was hard to adjust to having a meaningful dating relationship. It looked like stress. All. The. Time.

When she decided to take the leap back into dating, Sarah became more dependent than she anticipated. After all, she had been out of practice for years. She became more fearful of rejection than before. There was a bond she needed to chase, but she couldn't go all in. She called herself a chameleon because she warped into whatever the other person was into in order to make herself more likeable by their standards. When her new haircut or outfit didn't work, she panicked. She fell into a deep despair, where she questioned her self-worth and tried to remember why she even chased this person at all. Her major conflict was between her resolve to be alone and the draw of another spirit. Sarah genuinely struggled with describing an ideal relationship because she hadn't seen one. Even the ones on TV were unattainable, as far as she was concerned.

Resentment. It's an emotion fueled by the bitterness of feeling treated unfairly, and is what a lot of women harbor toward their fathers in some way. Wherever they find themselves on the spectrum, there is self-doubt, lack of security, disappointment and rage, all wrapped up in one. It bleeds over into their interactions with other people. Yet, there is a glimmer of hope in the most painful part of sessions. For the woman willing to come to grips with the issue that is outside of them, there is such a weight lifted. The work allows us to distribute responsibility where it is due. There is a chance for us to become attached to the real Father who matters, even if the one we were given here on Earth sucks.

EIGHT

Self-Care Check-In

1. Which attachment style do you identify with and why?
2. How is this influenced by your DI symptoms?
3. What was your inner child like? What did she feel like most of the time? What did she need to be happy? Did she dream?

Activity:

Write a letter to your inner child. Tell her who you are now. Tell her what you learned and how you are excited for her future! Let her know your successes and that even though you may have had missteps, she will be ok.

NINE

Heavenly Father vs. Earthly Father

I tried to write a book that didn't include overt references to God. Foolishly, I believed I could hide the God in me so I didn't offend anyone. That's my bad. If you're reading this, chances are you've heard the story of Christianity: God comes down from heaven as a man, Jesus Christ, to sacrifice himself for our sins. So, now we can live a life filled with grace and the chance of eternal life if we accept Christ, believing He died for us and rose again. This is called the Gospel.

On the flip side, I'm aware that spiritual abuse exists. Some people use religious doctrine or spirituality to enforce unhealthy ideals, as a means of controlling others. This obviously inflicts physical, emotional and mental damage. Many of us have come into some kind of contact with spiritual abuse at some point.

My experience in working with people revealed that believing in something larger than us is part of what gives us hope. For Christians, our moral compasses are born from the lessons we glean from the Bible. To that end, I want to make it clear that we do not have a monopoly on being good people. Yes, you can still be an amazing person and have a totally different philosophy on life. To a large extent, our values are shaped by religion, spirituality, or lack thereof. It all depends. There are so many lessons that are informed by these existential questions about existence and how the universe plays a role.

Regardless of one's belief system, God looks different to everyone. Even if I have a similar belief with another Christian, we still find some nuanced divergence in our understanding. Clients tell me that they hold on to the fact that God must be trying to teach them something, that God is trying to redirect their paths with various obstacles. There's also the idea that God exists to punish us for doing wrong and this condemnation is what keeps us humble. There are so many stories in between. I am fascinated by the way people conceptualize God. For example, there is much conversation about the difference between religion and spirituality, where the former is based on rules and rituals that put God in a box. I consider myself more spiritual as I get older. I understand grace. I no longer view God in a punitive way because I finally built a relationship where I believe in the possibility of unconditional love.

When I engaged in counseling, my own therapist delivered a mindblowing reality to me about my DI: the way I conceptualized God was a direct reflection of my experience with my earthly, biological father. Check it.

It took at least 20 years to get to the point I am in my spiritual walk. I had a mental block all that time. When I finally decided to explore what was getting in the way, I found that the issues came back to how I was taught by the spiritual leader in my family, my dad. I learned who God was through his actions and what he told us. I took away negative messages, that God punishes us when we do bad things. The negative consequences my dad doled out were a lot like what I imagined God would do. Daddy was like a god in that he made the rules. But, unlike God, we didn't have a choice of whether or not to do as we were told.

Naturally, when I thought of God, I had a certain vision based on who I interacted with daily. I saw him as a huge, finger-waving, white man with long hair sitting in the clouds scrutinizing my every move. My dad isn't a white man; the media I watched gave me that picture. Regardless, I was convinced he would punish me for even thinking the wrong thoughts. It got so bad that when I heard a curse word I thought I needed to ask forgiveness for putting myself in a setting where people said such things!

It was like waiting for lightning to strike at all times. Daddy will always be a no-nonsense type of guy. My brother and I learned pretty quickly that it was Daddy's way or no way; he dared us to question it. Let me clarify, I didn't grow up in a physically abusive home. I wasn't verbally abused by him as a young child. But there was something about Daddy that didn't allow me to feel confident in voicing my opinion. You know the story: kids are not encouraged to question their parents about anything. They aren't supposed to do anything that may embarrass them. By that logic, it was easy to feel unsupported growing up.

Mr. P was my band teacher in 6th grade. I loathed him. As a middle school-aged girl, I was coming into my own, having now become beautifully skilled at playing the flute. I practiced a lot at home and became first chair, but one of the only things that got in the way of my greatness was my "bad attitude." My side-eye stare could melt people. My pent-up anger had a lot to do with what I was dealing with at home. By middle school, my parents were separating. Daddy was no longer in the house. Although I had a fearful love for my father and was glad that tension was over, I still missed him. It was a confusing time!

Mr. P would trigger the crap out of me when he targeted me for certain behaviors such as talking, even when I wasn't the only student talking. I was always in trouble. He demoted me several chairs down for it, no matter how good I was. Despite my "bad attitude," I knew where to draw the line. I wasn't the kid to get written up or suspended. Remember, this is the girl who got her last beating before even setting foot in elementary school! I knew better. I like to think my attitude was misinterpreted. I was learning to assert myself. Perhaps it was a lot to attempt for a 12 year old, but I was just starting to be my own advocate in the face of injustice. Some of the adults around me didn't care that I was trying to figure out how to do this in a tactful manner. I didn't deserve to be treated that way in front of the whole class, day in and out. The guy had it out for me.

One afternoon, Mr. P told me to put my instrument away and sit out for the rest of class. I complied, but I wasn't going to do so without using my time wisely. I sat there and wrote him a letter. It was a scathing review of how he treated me unfairly and that his attitude was unacceptable. I gave him examples of how much he needed me to make the sound come together and told him punishing me this way was counterproductive. I let Mr. P know I would only become worse if he kept singling me out. I wanted him to know he was hurting the band, but also that I really enjoyed being there and he was hurting me as well. I had to be heard. We had had too many run-ins by then where I was left feeling embarrassed and devalued. Mr. P's behavior was reminiscent of how Daddy treated me at home. I would speak up, only to be told my opinion didn't matter and to stay in a child's place. It was like living out the tension from home and bringing it to school.

When my parents got wind of what happened, they met with Mr. P, and during the meeting my dad simply nodded and looked at me with utter disappointment. He heard Mr P describe my behaviour and call it a disruption. I was ticked off, but Daddy was there, so I knew better than to express it. After the meeting I was grounded. The small luxuries I had were taken away. These things didn't matter as much as my dad telling me that I shouldn't have dared speak to a teacher in that manner. He asked me, "Who do you think you are?" I hate that question. It's so demeaning to have someone demand you lower your growing self-esteem to meet their debased standard for you, or themselves. Instead of asking my side of the story, assumptions were made. Daddy believed a virtual stranger over me. I wasn't given any advice on how to deal with jerks like Mr. P; there was no discussion of what to do when I was faced with difficult personalities. I was expected to just shut up. I was supposed to be quiet because Daddy had the final word.

I felt defeated once I returned to class. There may have been another two times I did the same thing. I had a problem letting things go; this process is ongoing. I eventually gave up. I had tried to stand up for myself and assert my word, but it was looked at in a negative light. Many children deal with this kind of early silencing, which affects their ability to stand up in the face of important issues. Acting out in class is truly a cry for help. I know, you've heard this before. Some of you may believe this to be an excuse. But I would beg to differ. Regardless of the way the emotions come out in certain behaviors, good or bad, those feelings are valid. They are coming from a real place. They inspire our actions. There I was, with yet another experience of feeling unsupported by a man who was essentially modeling who God was for me.

Imagine that same defeated young girl going to church the Sunday after the parent-teacher meeting. I was always told God was the guy who would have my back regardless of my wrongdoing. I knew how to pray by then; it was, and still is, just talking to God. I asked Him why things turned out the way they did. I wondered why I got in trouble. I prayed to never feel that level of discomfort again and to feel loved by my dad instead. That level of disappointment from a parent can be crushing. Although I knew I had my mother's unconditional love, children have a funny way of pining for the absent parent. It was almost as if it didn't matter that my mom was there. I wanted to impress my dad. I wanted to know what it was like to have him appreciate me. I didn't know what it felt like to make my dad proud.

This warped lens was all I had to work with to build a relationship with God. I asked myself, "If I'm worshiping this God, shouldn't He have shown up when my parents were separating? Shouldn't I have felt loved and appreciated?"

Red and yellow, black and white;

We are precious in his sight;

Jesus loves the little children of the world!

Is this true for me? I wondered. *Are there too many kids for God to look after? Am I getting lost in translation?* There are so many theories on the subject of spiritual development. In general, these theories point back to how we evolved from having a primitive, survival mindset to learning to incorporate a higher power that answers questions larger than us. Spirituality is one of the ways we anchor the anxiety of not knowing how things happen and why we tick the way we do.

My parents' separation was a huge turning point in my understanding of religion and spirituality.This is where I began to question things. Like many kids, my brother and I were in church because we had to be. It was certainly part of our survival, in that it was an expectation in our home. Everything we learned about God was from my dad. He was instrumental in helping my mom come to Jesus before they were married, so he took the job as our family shepherd, like many other Christian homes with the father at the helm. After years of Sunday school and praying together, we could grasp the gospel but it didn't stick. How could it? All the positive feelings of the Bible stories were clouded by our dad's authoritarian ways. It was not easy to see God as a loving father when the support I had from my own felt conditional. There was a huge conflict I wasn't sure I would ever reconcile.

When our spiritual captain moved out, we spent less time at church. It felt weird at first. We had developed a tradition of being there regularly. I was under the impression that I would feel God only when I was in the building. But, having equated God with Daddy to an extent, I was happy to remove Him from the house along with Daddy. My mother worked a lot. Free of Daddy, she began to discover partying and lived her best life. We were physically taken care of between the two of them, but it was a huge adjustment for our family. Given the choice, I had no interest in going to church. There was no point, as far as I was concerned. After all, a relationship with God represented negative judgment and expectations I could do without.

By the time I got to college, I no longer attended church at all. I partied instead. Some people do both: get loose on Saturday and get up in time to go to the House of the Lord Sunday. I prefered to sleep in. There were Bible studies I could have joined, but I just prayed my way through things on my own for important events like passing a test because I didn't study, getting a cutie's attention, not wrecking the car on my "drive of shame" when I was hungover. I didn't need anyone else shoving their ideals down my throat. I knew I wasn't living a morally upstanding life, but I was having fun.

At least, that's what I told myself. Clearly, I was rebelling. I had never experienced freedom like this. Like many freshmen who realized their parents weren't there to check them, I went to school and went bananas! Moreover, Daddy wasn't around. Even with him being out of the house since I was in middle school, he managed to get reports of what I was doing around town throughout high school. So, being an hour away from home was a relief. There was something about not having him in the same city that took a major load off.

I had also convinced myself I was hiding from God in a way. I had come closer to equating my earthly father with my heavenly father. Putting them in the same category was easy: they were both men who had abandoned me in several ways. Both were figures who were supposed to be loving and available, yet it was hard to feel their presence.

It took a while to admit that I was mad at God. I never got the answers about why my parents didn't get back together. I'm almost ashamed to say I was hanging on to hope that they would. I didn't like coming from a broken home. I had worked hard not to be a statistic in other ways. I was the accomplished Black girl from a background of financial and familial struggle who's made it to college despite the odds! I figured being another girl without a dad tainted my record. I was embarrassed and frustrated. If anyone mentioned the goodness of God, I scoffed. *Yea, right. Where was He when...,* I thought. These thoughts intensified when, a year into college, I learned something that shocked me to my core.

THE DAY my Life Shifted

By the end of my sophomore year, problems with my dad came to a head. We were at each other's throats about a number of issues. I was becoming more vocal about things that bothered me, especially since he started seriously dating another woman. The distance between us was intensifying. It was as if there was something in the air that nobody was telling me.

I can't recall the premise of our argument. I can only remember how I felt on that fateful day. I was in my mother's apartment pulsating with rage after speaking with him. Mommy looked at me with a blank stare. She was annoyingly silent. Looking back, I realize she was fearful about what she knew she needed to do.

"Christian, I need to tell you something," Mommy said in an uncharacteristically timid way.

"What? Is Daddy not my real dad?" The words just came out of my mouth. You may know the story of the talking donkey in the Bible. God used it to send a message to the man that was riding him. I'm sure it was just as freaky that this donkey spoke. My words just formed that day; I was thinking how impossible it was that I had come from such a person.

"How did you know?" my mom replied. She couldn't continue. The only noise in the room was her crying, confirming a line I'd tossed out in an angry rant.

I learned that the man who raised me might not be my biological father. I will never forget the questions that followed this revelation. Most of them were surrounding my identity. *Who am I? Where had I inherited the defiance that brewed inside me for so long? Was that from another family? How was I to act? Think? Who do I watch for guidance now? Who do I believe?*

Although I loved my mother, she had lied to me for so long. Should I trust her because she produced receipts? They say better late than never. My mom told me that she had responded to Daddy's mistreatment by sleeping with another person for revenge, a man we will call "Dean". I was about 2 years old when she dropped the bomb on my dad. They raised me another 16 years knowing I may not be Daddy's daughter.

"I want to go see him, take me to the guy," I demanded.

It turned out he had lived in the same place for the last 19 years. I didn't shed a tear the entire ride there. When we pulled up to Dean's house, my mom went to knock on the door. Dean answered it with a smile.

"I wondered if I was ever going to meet you," he said to me.

Dean had basically been waiting on me for almost 20 years, hoping that this day would come. He had been living with his own questions as well. This is where I lost it. I cried and ran back to the car, overwhelmed.

I called my dad the next day. He wanted to continue our argument from before, but I had no more fight in me. I let him talk.

"And you know what? This is going to blow your mind. You may not--" he started.

"...even be your daughter? I know. Mommy told me yesterday. I actually guessed it," I cut him off. He thought he had one up on me so I slam-dunked the point before he could use it to hurt me.

"Oh, of course y'all talked about it," he retorted. It seemed to bother him that he missed his chance to drop the bomb, to deliver the news to end my self-worth single handedly.

I got to know my potential biological father in the days following. My mom, Dean, and I would go out for drinks and tell stories from the old days. I learned he had kept tabs on me my entire life. He knew I was in the band and that I considered running track in high school. It was nice to know he was interested. It was also sad that he couldn't be there the way he wanted to out of concern for causing any damage. After about two months, we all got the courage and took a paternity test.

It was not a match. Now, I really felt like an orphan. I wasn't sure how to take this news back to my dad because we weren't on speaking terms. Dean and I never spoke again. God had played another cruel trick on me, I thought. Just when I had a chance at a decent relationship with a father who wanted to be invested, he was taken from me. And so, my image of God was tainted again. Sadly, the inconsistency of His presence felt in line with what my dad did next: refused to take a paternity test.

"I knew it wasn't going to be a match," he said, almost triumphantly. "I already took a test years ago when I found out," Daddy continued.

I tried to ignore it and yet, I couldn't let it go. "Why can't you tell me the results? Or you could just take it again. I don't get how this type of information can just get lost. It doesn't make sense," I cried.

"I'm not taking it again. I'm not about to be in the line up with a bunch of niggas your momma slept with. *I* know the results; and that's for *me* to know," Daddy told me. "I raised you because it was the right thing to do," he said. Not because he loved me.

He was done with it. He wasn't going to reveal the results...*if* he took the test in the first place. I begged him to change his mind ten years later; his tune remained the same.

It wasn't until very recently that I found the answer to my paternity. My brother was gracious enough to take a DNA test, which would produce results saying we were either half or whole siblings. Since we know we have the same mother, it was the next best thing. I was happy to learn the man I'm writing about is indeed my biological father! I feel free and empowered! But I am still thoroughly disappointed that I had to take matters into my own hands without any of his help. At the time of me writing this book, my father hasn't spoken to me regarding the positive results I shared with him. For a while, he was the one person who had the key to my paternity; he can no longer hold this over my head. This seems more important to him than a relationship at this point. It's an extremely hurtful thing to know the man who raised you doesn't believe you deserve to know who you are. Talk about abusing power and control!

Before learning the results with my brother, my entire self-worth was shot. I was operating like half a person. I didn't feel comfortable going to the doctor because I had half a family history now. It took 15 years before I set my first appointment for a check up since freshman year of college. I have been pregnant twice since then. But I went to doctor's visits with extreme anxiety, not knowing how my kids would turn out. I thought I knew myself, but I had lost an entire part of me.

The questionable paternity experience was a pivotal growth period for my spiritual walk. I didn't know how to see God as the wholesome, amazing God I know today. I learned complete abandonment after that, which ramped up my DI symptoms to a higher degree. Moreover, it blocked any sense of the gracious essence of God. I lost my sense of self and who I was because the father figure in my life didn't nurture a strong sense of self-worth; he reinforced low esteem by denying his biological association with me, or at least allowing me to hang in limbo. My dating life, marriage, friendships, work--everything was affected by this uncertainty of who I was.

As adults, we wonder why it's so difficult to use our voice in an effective manner. I treat people daily who weren't afforded the opportunity to exercise the muscles of voice and choice. Questioning my paternity certainly stole my voice. I couldn't imagine going places and commanding authority when I thought I was half a person. *Who would listen to me?* I thought. Think of how that could affect someone's view of God. Would we then feel it's OK to approach Him with concerns? If so, do we truly expect Him to answer our prayers or do we just ready ourselves for condemnation? These are tough questions for even the strongest believer. We want to be confident that He will prevail over all, but there's that inkling that He will fail us, just like our fathers. It makes me think of all the questions I have for Him about justice. *Won't He just let us down anyway? When will He show Himself? He's probably going to forget about me like my own father did.* The list of questions goes on. Even the most well-adjusted paternal relationships are impacted by lack of trust at some point.

So this revelation was facilitated through my therapist years later, that because God is presented as our father in the Christian faith, we conceptualize Him by way of our relationships with our earthly fathers. One way to address this issue is to give yourself permission to be mad at God. Question him with the most open, angry prayer you can. Habbakuk did. He is a little known prophet in the Bible who was so pissed at the situation around him, he wondered where God was. And he let God know he felt abandoned. He presented God with his own plan and everything (Habbakuk 1:2-4). Isn't that just like us? We have a better way to do things because we have a better "boots-on-the-ground" view. Despite this obviously flawed belief, God encourages us to test and question Him. In fact, the invitation is there in His word because He's provided yet another way, another reason to get closer to him. In Habbakuk's case, God answered with a simple, "I get it. I see you. I love you. Now watch me work." (Habbakuk 1:5-7).

Our Earthly fathers may not be this cool. Even if they are less authoritarian, there's always the temptation to enforce the power they know is present in the relationship dynamic. In my case, because of the authority that was established by my dad, I never felt comfortable questioning the powers that be. To overcome this, I had to revisit my perception of God and stop holding Him to a flawed, human standard.

I LIVED this out when I got pregnant. By then, I was 25 years old. Daddy and I hadn't spoken in a few years. I wasn't pressed to tell him anything about carrying Tony's child. I figured it would come with condemnation. So, I lived and prepared for our son. I started to go to church again. Despite the resistance I had for years up to that point, I knew there was something there for me. I needed a good Word. I needed healing from the pain I felt when I thought of my own father daily. I needed to feel cleansed and seen by the father everyone said wouldn't waver, even if it felt like that to us.

I remember walking into service on a Sunday morning at a small church. There was a welcoming atmosphere that made me feel safe. There were still the butterflies in my stomach, though. I almost felt naked walking in. It was a vulnerable place to be in: I was about 4 months along, my belly was showing, and I had no ring on my finger. I mentioned already how much that meant a lot in the Bible Belt. I was made to believe that it was a shameful thing to be an unwed mother. But I didn't let it stop me. I felt drawn to the space and the word I knew God would deliver to me. I was happy to be there.

My gut told me I was supposed to be there. Although, I have to admit, I was underwhelmed. *No matter*, I thought, *I am just trying to get in the swing of things.* My overall goal was to answer to that innate connection to God I knew was there. I supposed it was a good start. After service, the pastor called anyone up to the altar who wanted prayer. *This has got to be it,* I said to myself. The pastor was going down the line of everyone, giving a prophetic word to whomever he felt led. I was a bit uncomfortable, but I was planted, determined to stay for my Word. When he got to me, he looked me square in the eyes, "God wants you to hear this: He said He still knows you."

I was in tears immediately. I thought of all the times I thought I was alone when I did things I wasn't proud of. I remembered the times I felt like God couldn't possibly take me back. I was conditioned to think that way by a judgmental father who would surely turn up his nose at me. But I was getting the two confused. God wasn't the guy I grew up knowing in my house. I had made the mistake of bringing Him down to the human standard, where people let other people down all the time.

In that moment, an instant sense of calm took over my body. All this time, when I thought I had done too much to come back from, I realized I hadn't learned about grace yet. I still had the image of the man waving his finger at me for my transgressions--I saw my Earthly father. I finally understood, they weren't the same. And it was high time I started making moves toward the one I knew wanted to love me with all my flaws, one who would operate out of blatant, loving correction. I needed a break from all the times I was feeling less than in order to make someone else feel worth something.

. . .

SO, how do we escape the symptoms of DI? The work obviously starts with us; we have to be motivated, ready, and able to handle what comes out of difficult work like this. I turn to the ultimate example of a Father. We learn how His grace applies to our lives. This is literally one of my favorite things to talk about. We have access to the freely given, undeserved, unmerited love and favor of God by believing in the death, burial, and resurrection of Jesus Christ. That's literally it. When I do something I would normally beat myself up about, I don't have to worry about whether God will look at me with enough disapproval to take back His precious gift. This can be hard for a person with DI to get. It means that we can accept that screwing up doesn't come with a lecture or harsh judgment. Weird, right?

Self Care Check-in

1. Religion is about subscribing to a certain doctrine within the confines of rules and laws that can make us feel condemned if you miss grace. Spirituality is about connection with The Most High; it involves the connection to His creation, including nature and the universe. Do you consider yourself to be one or the other? If not, what do you consider to be your guiding light?

2. Do you believe your DI symptoms impact your conceptualization of a higher power?

3. Have your DI symptoms been improved or worsened by religion and/or spirituality? Why or why not?

**ACTIVITY:

Spend time in nature! Go for a walk or sit at the park. Kick your feet in the sand on a shore. Take a few deep breaths while you're there; you can close your eyes if you're comfortable. Notice three things you see, hear, smell, taste, and feel.

TEN

Self Care Check-in

1. Religion is about subscribing to a certain doctrine within the confines of rules and laws that can make us feel condemned if you miss grace. Spirituality is about connection with The Most High; it involves the connection to His creation, including nature and the universe. Do you consider yourself to be one or the other? If not, what do you consider to be your guiding light?
2. Do you believe your DI symptoms impact your conceptualization of a higher power?
3. Have your DI symptoms been improved or worsened by religion and/or spirituality? Why or why not?

Activity:

Spend time in nature! Go for a walk or sit at the park. Kick your feet in the sand on a shore. Take a few deep breaths while you're there; you can close your eyes if you're comfortable. Notice three things you see, hear, smell, taste, and feel.

ELEVEN

DI and Friendship

My first friend was my younger brother, Alex. I remember being very protective of him as kids and still find myself to be. Mommy told me she and my dad framed Alex's arrival as a new blessing for our house. They made sure I knew the exciting responsibility of being a big sister, and that I was going to be promoted to a helper--big girl status! I took that role seriously. I gave myself the tasks of shielding my new little brother from harm, helping my parents feed him, and keeping him entertained. We bonded immediately and became inseparable. I think it helped that we are only 16 months apart.

My brother has always been a special spirit, highly sensitive to his own emotions and insightful about others'. Alex was able to tell when I was upset and comforted me with silly songs he made up, or hugs. He seemed to be happy when I was. He was playful and continues to answer the urge to feed his inner child. He knew what he needed from an early age, but there were times when he was also stifled by the domineering nature of Daddy.

When it was time for one of his whoopings, I found myself too terrified to stand up for my brother. There was a conflict: do I advocate for my best and only friend? Or do I let it go to save myself? This turmoil became part of the way I conceived of friendship. I had an innate sense of loyalty to my brother. I knew the importance of having someone's back right away. Unfortunately, Daddy made it clear what it would cost if I did so. My fear of getting a whooping or having something taken away kept me quiet and weakened my conflict resolution skills, which didn't help later when I would encounter disagreements with peers. I found myself choosing friendships where I played a supportive role. I didn't think I would be listened to in social settings either. It's amazing what a kid picks up in the FOO, right?

Alex was an ally in the struggle. It was helpful to have someone around experiencing the same family dynamic. My brother and I obviously had different perspectives. What I interpreted as hurtful or scary, he was able to brush off with a confidence I wish I had. Like my father, he moved with a swagger that commanded a room. His very aura was calming and sure. He even looks like Daddy--dead ringer. Once, my grandmother found an 8th grade school picture of Daddy, wearing a powder blue suit and an innocent smile. The resemblance between him and Alex is uncanny! To this day, they share strong characteristics, from the way they exchange a look to their laughs. The resemblance only goes so far, though. Alex loves our mother to death, and he showed his appreciation for her growing up. His actions gave me a glimpse into how a woman should be loved, and were a qualifying factor for choosing friends. I wanted someone who would validate me as much as he did.

As kids, I think our varying opinions helped us practice using our voices and talking about our frustrations. In our own language, we knew when and what we needed as we learned to navigate the world by way of our little family. The closeness in age helped, as we vibed because of our common interests in our favorite cartoons and learning new things together. We used to play a game where we would pick a destination anywhere in the world. We weren't the best at geography, but we knew that the trip would be way more fun if we went far away. We would be in our shared room, packing up all the things we needed for our road trip. Eventually our cars (twin beds) would be packed to the hilt with all the essentials: shoes, clothes, toys, toilet paper, and snacks. It was so fun to imagine travelling with my brother, seeing the world beyond the chaos that sometimes engulfed our house. We spent most of the day playing these games until I got old enough to enter elementary school.

I went to kindergarten, which interrupted a huge chunk of our time together. It was a tough transition for both of us. I was in a different world with other kids who played unique games. My teachers were sharing things with me I hadn't seen before. It was exciting! The plus side was that I could come home and share these new revelations with my brother. The down side was that I missed him.

By the time I was in first grade, Alex had enrolled in the same school. We were in completely different halls, but I felt closer to him. By then I was slowly coming into my own, having been in the mix with other kids for a year. My brother was struggling a little. I will never forget the first time he found his way to my classroom during the day. There I was, coloring or something, and I turned around to see Alex's head peeking into the door.

"And who do you belong to?" My teacher, Mrs. G, asked him. She was so sweet about it.

"Brishtan," he said, pointing in my direction. I had been working with him to correct his pronunciation for a while.

"Boy! What are you doing here?" I said with a laugh.

He had somehow snuck away from his kindergarten hall and found me. Mrs. G was nice enough to allow me to walk him back to his classroom. On the way there, Alex told me how much he wanted to be near me instead of in his new classroom. Like a good big sister, I promised him I would see him when we got home, where we could hang out and play our favorite games together. It took awhile for him to get used to his new setting--so close, being in the same building, but still so far from me. That wasn't the last time he randomly appeared in my classroom. And every time, I would walk him back, hand in hand.

Daddy issues looked different for my brother, as mental health symptoms present a little differently for men. However, it's important to note that DI symptoms also have implications for nonsexual intimate relationships. Recall that the symptoms include an overall sense of insecurity, questioning one's decisions and self worth deficits. There is also a need for validation in friendships. Let's explore how DI shows up here.

The Needy Friend

If we consider the "Clingy Type" of woman with DI symptoms and insecure attachment, we have unlocked key ingredients for the "Needy Friend." This woman is likely highly sensitive to her anxious thought spirals that tell her she isn't being "fun enough," "smart enough," "cool enough," or "supportive enough." It's like living under pressure to perform.

Imagine the lack of secure attachment present for this friend. She is likely engaging in things she doesn't want to do in order to keep the relationship intact, be it attending parties or going kayaking just for the sake of friendship. This woman loses herself in the friendship, hence the iffy attachment issues. When her girlfriends try to introduce other people, the Needy Friend is going to respond in a jealous way. She may not want to share. It is not a far reach to consider that this woman may have experienced abandonment on some level from her father.

Keisha came into my office in a rant one day. Her session started out pretty intensely.

"Dis hoe on IG out with these other bitches without me," she said. No, I didn't have a chance to say hello. She was ready to get right to it.

"I take it you have a problem with your friend spending time with other people. It's all in your body language and tone, sis," I responded. I noticed how her anxiety presented: heavy breathing, fast-talking and her right leg was shaking.

"Nah, she was just telling me she don't trust nobody. She told me she only talks to me about the 'real shit.' What the hell they got to talk about for a whole weekend and I ain't there?" Keisha's anxiety was presenting as anger.

Her relationships with other people went pretty much the same way. It was interesting that she could be friends with all these people, but they were not allowed to branch out. To do so meant a hurtful level of disloyalty to Keisha. She felt the need to call, text and email multiple times when she didn't get a response. The stories she made up in her head were about threats to her friendships. She and I did a lot of digging into her thoughts and feelings about her father.

Keisha and her brother had been without their father for a few years after their parents separated. She was about 10 years old when he left. She was hopeful that he would return and entertain a real father-daughter relationship, and he did, but he added someone else to the mix. It threw her for a loop.

"He got remarried. He was with this woman I barely knew. He ain't take any time to introduce her to me," she said. "It wasn't fair. I had done all this work to make sure we were working on our relationship once he had come back in our lives again."

Keisha's trust issues stemmed from a myriad of things, but she credits her father's intermittent presence as part of the equation. She vowed to make every friendship she had count, but wasn't ready to let anyone else in who could jeopardize a "good thing." She and I had to work on building a healthy view of what she brought to the table and trust that not everyone was out to get her. Her neediness was rooted in a fear that she would be hurt again. We worked with this to help point to ways she could fill the voids she identified in a healthy way.

The HWIC

The Head Woman In Charge is a boss. Sometimes, she can be known as the mean girl because she wants what she wants when she wants it...and she isn't afraid to let people know. She can be the "Daddy's Girl" and "Gold Digger" on the extreme part of the scale. Her communication can be unfiltered and aggressive. On the flip side, she can also be the one who brings people together. People may look to her for guidance in certain situations for her wisdom because, after all, she knew everyone first and is well-versed in how to mitigate disagreements.

Either way, there is a take-charge attitude embedded in her DNA. She's the leader of the friend group, whether as the glue that holds the group together or the one who isn't afraid to speak up for one of her friends. She likely honed these skills by watching a father run the household a certain way. Her DI symptoms may show up as domineering traits. There is a certain level of anxiety she has that forces her to control everything around her.

I knew a girl like this in the first grade. I'll never forget Frances; she was a brat. She spoke to her parents like they were minions, present only to do her bidding. I once went to her house to complete a project, and her mother prepared sandwiches and snacks for us. Frances went nuts when her mother didn't have the spread she wanted! I wouldn't have dared talk to my mother that way. Because of his busy work schedule, her dad had instilled in her a huge sense of entitlement. He threw whatever she wanted her way to compensate for his absence.

When we were in school, I damn sure wasn't trying to be her friend. I watched her with other kids. She was just as entitled with them and bossed them around. She had definitely transferred her "Queen of the Castle" attitude to the playground. Even with that attitude, she managed to have a consistent following.

The Flake

We all have this friend. The woman who doesn't follow through on anything she says she will do. It's such a pet peeve of mine! You ask her to braid your hair because she's good and doesn't charge you, but she cancels...even when you plan to give her something for her troubles anyway! Maybe she doesn't text back for days. The list goes on.

The Flake is reminiscent of the *anxious-avoidant* attachment type we discussed earlier. Someone with this level of attachment is not trying to fully commit for fear of getting hurt. There's a conflict where the person is almost sure a friendship is beneficial, but knows they have a duty to protect themselves at all costs.

Our flaky friend likes to ride the fence and have options because she likely learned that having plans A-Z is helping her address her anxiety. Yes, ladies. The root of the flake is a certain level of concern with how attaching to people will play out, especially if she had a father in the house who showed her that she was an option instead of a priority. We know by now that we are the products of our environments. So, it's entirely possible that the Flaky Friend is just that way because of what she saw her father do. She adapted so that she doesn't get hurt. It's a defense mechanism for her to avoid engaging/investing in relationships that would be potentially harmful, despite how it makes her look. When it comes down to it, emotional safety is the priority.

The User

Rashida was a former client of mine. She lived by an interesting commandment: *Thou shalt get them, before thou art got.* Nothing was more true for how she operated in life. Each person she came into contact with on a nonsexual level was strictly business; she didn't participate in intimate relationships.

When I asked her about her DI, she said very matter-of-factly, "I get in and I get out. I don't need friends." She shared that her father was a man who liked to wheel-and-deal, as they say. He was usually involved in a get-rich-quick scheme a few times a year, which led to Rashida witnessing him swindle people left and right.

"He would sell this and that. He always wanted to make sure he was around people who could benefit him, didn't think about how it would be the other way around," Rashida told me.

It was interesting to me that she had someone for everything she needed. She called them "hookups." She had someone she could grab coffee with when she was bored, she knew who to call if she had questions about a certain business venture, people she would party with.

"All these interactions seem to have potential for friendships," I told her. "How do you keep that from happening?"

"I self-sabotage things," she said. It was what her last therapist had pointed out to her. "It's not something I am proud of. It became a knee-jerk reaction when I met someone," she told me. Her insight was on point.

After a few months of getting what she needed, the relationship would self-destruct. There was a cycle she was trying to break. She knew it wasn't healthy. But she didn't know how to handle relationships that involved a certain level of vulnerability on her part. I learned more about her relationship with her father. Her interactions with him were transactional: he would give her time in exchange for her involvement in guilting friends and family into his sales schemes. This meant she had the role of leaking certain things about not having things she needed so people would feel obligated to support her father's latest venture. Rashida learned a valuable skill set; we all need to learn to sell ourselves at some point. But she missed the lessons on a reciprocal, more intimate exchange.

The famous Greek philosopher Aristotle wrote about friendships. He outlined three different types: friendships of utility, friendships of pleasure, and friendships of good. Rashida exercised friendships of utility, where she would have superficial relationships with people, using them for what they had to offer. It is obviously the type that doesn't stand the test of time. Friendships of pleasure are those that are based out of common interests between people. This sounds good, but it's only a start. One can't rely on common interests alone. These relationships don't last either, as interests change and people grow. Good, virtuous exchanges between people who share legitimate, mutual respect and appreciation for one another's qualities is what makes a true friendship (CITE: https://medium.com/@iantang/3-kinds-of-friends-you-meet-in-life-6b03c8383a85)

The lack of security found in DI symptoms can greatly cloud the innate draw to others' positive qualities. If one's worldview is warped in a way that disallows trust of the self and those around them, it is obviously difficult to forge healthy friendships.

When I got to fourth grade, I found a friendship that I still cherish. Jessica and I bonded over our love for my first boy band obsession, Immature. Our connection started with common interests, but we evolved together over the years. At her house I felt safe and heard; I could focus on having fun instead of listening to the arguments my parents had. By the time we were in sixth grade together, we met our third best friend, Michele. Our crew, MCJ, was inseparable and I loved that I had two sisters who validated me. This is where I learned to reciprocate love in a new way. I need you to hear me: When given the right opportunities, when you have the willingness to be vulnerable, you can be unstoppable. We went from being little girls to women together. They changed my life and I love them dearly.

I learned that these friendships were different from the one with my brother, where we fought and made up. At home with him, those fights would look a lot like the ones between my parents: yelling and slamming of things. The disagreements my brother and I had quickly escalated because we didn't have a healthy way to address the discomfort we felt physically and emotionally. We would eventually resolve the trivial disagreement of what to watch on TV together, but I would still be left unsettled. I am sure it affected my brother too.

Learning that arguments got worse when I was older scared me. It was inevitable that this type of situation would arise between my new best friends and me. I wondered if I would lose them because I had not learned how to speak my piece when I disagreed. I certainly didn't feel comfortable going to my parents; they barely knew how to do that themselves. I was anxious about the possibility of fighting in MCJ; what if they replace the "C"...me? I had found something special, so I resolved to let things slide. I was quite passive, although there was rarely a heated topic among MCJ.

Our relationship thrived on getting along and finding the same things in common. That was as far as my conceptualization of friendship went. I didn't know how to properly resolve any conflict then, so I had to go with what I knew: go with the flow and discount my thoughts and feelings that went against the grain. Looking back, I know MCJ's friendship would have been fine if I'd disagreed strongly on something. We held a safe space for each other. I was able to get my feet wet in the pool of honesty with them, but I went only so far. I had found a good thing. I didn't want to be without them. You could call me the Needy Friend at that point.

MCJ taught me to be vulnerable over the years. But my own lessons about friendship still needed tweaking. I was coming up on an opportunity to learn even more about meeting new people: it was time for us to go to college. Jessica decided to venture off hundreds of miles away from us. I felt disappointed in her decision. I knew she would go far being such a genius, but it also felt like a personal attack. My DI symptoms flared and the insecurities reared their heads. *Am I not a good enough friend to make her want to stay? I thought we would go to college together. Will she remember to call?* I had several thought spirals going in the wrong direction. I got over it, eventually. We have to give ourselves time to grieve our old selves. Change is hard, but we must respect the transition, as it only stands to make us better if we pay attention. Thankfully, I was going to college with Michele, who would be my roommate for the next 6 years after graduating high school.

Preparing to leave for undergrad produced a ball of emotions. I knew I would be leaving my pretty-much grown brother at home with Mommy. There was barely any support from our dad--at least emotionally. By then, Alex was his own man with friendships he chose. He was changing, having experienced his own trials with Daddy. Alex and I had a different relationship now, one that was more mature. Our discussions about Daddy were more involved, we had a larger emotional vocabulary to express our opinions on what went wrong in our family.

Mommy and Daddy had been separated for years now, they had both moved on. Alex was living with a friend instead of in the house with Mommy and me. It started as a sleepover one weekend, then every weekend, which eventually spilled over into weeks of him being gone. Since he moved on first, I remember feeling sad that our little unit had changed so much, but relieved that he was able to find solace in the new space. Fall 2004 was my new beginning; it was time for me to move on too. I was about to have my chance of freedom from the drama that went on. Daddy came to my high school graduation that spring. It was one of the few things he participated in. But I was happy he was there, nonetheless. I was leaving my young ways behind to become a new woman!

College was a whole mood, as the kids say. There was a huge shift from being around several dozen classmates in high school to people all over the state, country and even international. What a culture shock! I took this as an opportunity to dive in with both feet: I joined clubs right away to meet other people. I dragged Michele out to things so we could mingle with cute boys. It was fun getting exposure to diversity. As I was getting to know fellow coeds, I thought it would be beneficial to keep my formula the same: go with the flow, don't rock the boat. There were times I would think I was protecting my new friendship by agreeing with things I didn't or being someone I wasn't. Even the safest places I found in them wasn't enough for me to use my voice.

Like a lot of young adults trying to find their way, I bent to the needs of those around me to avoid conflict because, in my case, I knew I couldn't handle it. It didn't help that my dad's judgmental voice was in my head. I remember how he spoke about people who used drugs, drank, partied all night, etc. How they would never go anywhere and it wasn't any way to live. While I was stuck with that in my thought loop, I remembered one major point: he wasn't there. So that meant it was time to turn up!

From one frat party to the next, Michele and I travelled around meeting new people and becoming acquaintances with folks we ran into regularly. By then, she and I developed a clique of girls on our freshman dorm hall. We would hang out in each other's rooms, study together, and ride around our small college town, crowded in one of the two cars our new friends were allowed to have on campus. I took it upon myself to start drinking alcohol, which I'd tried one time the year before at a senior year kick-off party. Shots of Everclear and "Syzurp," a concoction of candy, vodka, cough medicine and fruit juice, were part of the norm on weekends. It was fun, but wouldn't have been my choice of a good time every time we hung out.

Regardless, I felt validated. When I was reinforced as the "fun" friend, I was getting a boost to the low self-esteem I came to college with. It was as if I was learning more ways to get and keep friends. Not to mention, part of the motive behind partying was to piss my dad off, but also prove him wrong: I could be successful even if I partied like the typical college kid. This is what I told myself. Even as an official adult, I knew better than to tell him these things. There I was again, silenced, unable to voice my opinion or be ready for the slightest conflict.

Sophomore year finally gave me an opportunity to see how I fared in an argument with a friend. I had a major disagreement with a girl who stayed on the same hall. I can't even remember what the blow-up was about. I just knew it was drama that went on for more than a month before we finally confronted each other about it. I can remember like yesterday, we came into my dorm room and I stood up on my bed, yelling at her and a mutual acquaintance of ours (yes, she brought back-up). I was surprised, betrayed, annoyed, furious. Praise God, Michele was there. She was privy to the drama and able to help me clean up my words.

I needed this support because I know my message got lost in the delivery. My points were valid, my feelings relevant and real, but I was a rookie in this area. All I had to go by was a black or white type of reaction to disagreements: either I was going to avoid it at all costs or I would go all the way in. This is what I was taught. There was no in between when my parents had a disagreement. Sometimes, Daddy belittled Mommy, then she would leave us, storming out into the night. This method of pissing someone off stuck with me. I knew how to hurt someone's feelings in a disagreement: yell and scream until you get your point across. If it wasn't clear, badger them until your point makes sense. If they are still too dumb to get it, storm out. My inner narrative told me I needed to kill or be killed, a message I learned from my dad telling us our whole lives that disrespect (especially toward him) was intolerable. Little did I know, I could have handled situations with grace and poise.

As a kid I loved Daddy's closest friends, who he'd known since high school: Roy, Brandon, and Trent. My brother called them our uncles. Uncle Roy had a son named Jason, who my brother and I played with when we travelled to their house. We visited as frequently as we could and I looked forward to the visits. Uncle Roy's wife, Latasha, was from London, so part of the excitement was hearing her foreign accent. Latasha would cook for us when we came. She made this amazing dish with ham, mushrooms, and some kind of cheese. It was like nothing I'd ever tasted. Thinking of Uncle Roy's house brings fond memories. It was going well for a while.

Suddenly, our monthly road trips to Greenville to visit Uncle Roy and his family stopped. I would hear Daddy talking crap about Uncle Roy. *I thought they were friends*, I pondered to myself. The visits left a void because trips to see him or having him stop by were part of life. After considerable time went by, we learned Uncle Roy was struggling with an issue, but instead of nurturing him through it, we heard Daddy talk down our uncle instead. Uncle Roy had done things that Daddy thought was putting our family in danger and I think he was setting a necessary boundary. At least, that's how he framed it. It was his responsibility to protect us, after all. But, to my brother and me, relegated as we were to staying in a child's place, Uncle Roy was just cut off.

Our Uncle Brandon was hilarious. My brother and I loved to laugh at his jokes. He and Daddy would go back and forth with funny quips. This was part of some of the good times in our home. Daddy described him as a man who couldn't get his life together. Uncle Brandon had a new job every three months. Something about this and other things didn't jive well with our dad. He didn't respond to people who weren't meeting his standard. He did the same thing to Uncle Brandon, cut him off and suddenly, my brother and I were mourning another loss.

Uncle Trent was a talented musician. He lived with his mother in the same house he'd grown up in. I don't know what the deal was with that, but I knew Daddy disapproved. It was made obvious by the things he would say behind Uncle Trent's back, though he was bold enough to tell all his friends what he thought to their faces. That was none of my business. What was my business, however, was how he presented these relationships to my brother and me. He was teaching us the value of friendship, whether he actually sat us down and had a conversation or not. We watched how he allowed 20 years of friendship between the three of them end in what felt like an instant. I'm quite sure things were brewing between the men, and every story has three sides: yours, theirs, and the truth. However, this is where we return to the FOO premise; we learn our quirks from our parents. Period.

Recall the "User" friend type. Their experiences have led to an idea of closeness which prevents a healthy development of trust, and therefore intimate relationships. This is what landed my dad in this category. I know now that my dad's issues likely presented in his friendships and contributed to their demise. In turn, I was left with no compass on how to navigate friendships. There was an opportunity for him to show his children that gaslighting (when the dominant person in a relationship makes the other person feel like they're making up things in their head, even when the dominant person is clearly sowing self-doubt) and deflection is unhealthy. But in his marriage to my mother, where kids see their first examples of friendships, and in his close friendships, he demonstrated unproductive ways to resolve conflict. Thankfully, I learned to reject some of his ideals and made lasting connections.

College gave me life-long friendships. I eventually learned I could disagree with others without fear of losing them. I even got to the point where I was alright if I didn't keep certain friendships. Adulting can be hard, but I am happy to report that I have an inner circle of great women who know the best and worst parts of me, DI and all! In fact, the concept of community is strong among friendships who share a struggle and can pour into each other in a positive way. Clearly, my idea of friendship evolved. I find myself calling them when I need to hear an uplifting word and I do the same for them.

The interesting thing about the friendships I have with each woman separately is that I don't feel intimidated anymore. As it turns out, I was battling with a level of insecurity that led me to feel inferior to people I met. This insecurity followed me through early adulthood, even when I found and established great friendships. I wondered if I was good enough to have such a great bond, one that would not require that I have something to offer other than myself. I didn't know it at the time, but God was helping me learn a special type of grace that friendships offer.

One of my close friends, Afton, taught me it was alright to just be me. Even after years of being friends with one of the most selfless people I know, Michele, I still found it difficult to accept the things Afton did for me. Be it lunch on her or borrowing her shoes; she helped me understand how to accept freely given gifts with no works, just being me. What a sweet gift! These type of messages became more clear as Jessica V., a sorority sister turned bestie, gave me gas money with no expectation of a reimbursement a few years ago. Or when Sauls, another soror, drove an hour away to my home to do my hair for my engagement shoot at no charge.

DI symptoms are real. They continue to be triggered by things around us, but they are treatable. We simply need the opportunities to exercise our decisions. We can relearn skill sets when we are in the right settings. I was presented with opportunities over the years that allowed me to exercise the muscle I hadn't spent time developing: my voice.

It was freeing! The feeling was so intoxicating that I would get ahead of myself sometimes. I had one of my friends tell me my energy can be intrusive. I suppose I can get carried away to the point of aggravation. When she told me, I was hurt, but she said so in love. It was something I needed to hear. I am still recalibrating how I interact with people and learning to be careful with others' perceptions. I am currently in the process of learning how to listen, when to engage, how to say anything, and what to say. I hear a lot of my dad coming out of me when I speak sometimes. It bothers me, but this is the first step to making positive changes and giving myself the grace I didn't always get as I ride this learning curve. I can be open with my friends about how my feelings are hurt or process the stories I make up in my head when they say or do certain things. I told one of my friends I felt blown off when she decided to do something else the weekend I planned fun for our sons to have a playdate. Turns out, all we needed was a conversation and we understood each other better. Back in the day, I would have believed our friendship was over because we disagreed.

Grace is one of the most simple concepts, but it is difficult to wrap my head around sometimes. Imagine being in a friendship that doesn't require that you work for anything. Jesus calls us his friend, but he's a legit higher power who is concerned with me. Little. Old. Me. I think the more I was able to grasp this concept rather than what I grew up with, the more I could get a handle on this friendship thing. God invites us to go to Him with prayer and petition. He answers lovingly. He understands I'm upset and yet, has the best plan for me. And still wants to be a friend and father to me in the best sense. It's amazing! I am not comparing my friends to God. But I find comfort in the fact that I believe he sent them to me to demonstrate the relationships he wants in my life. The kind that are authentic and force me to grow in spaces I didn't know I needed.

TWELVE

Self-Care Check-in

1. How do you define friendship? Where did you learn this definition? Think of your family of origin.
2. Friendship requires a certain level of trust. Think about the standard of trust in your friendships. Does this standard keep you safe? Why or why not?
3. How do you know when to set boundaries with unhealthy people?

Activity:

Think of who you want your friends to be. The following list will help you consider how to set standards for new people who come into your life, or help you set the boundaries with so-called friends. First, choose your top 5, then narrow it down to your top 3. These are your deal breakers and they will tell you a lot about who you invite into your circle. Think of how these people impact your needs when your DI symptoms increase.

1. Trust
2. Honesty
3. Loyalty
4. Vulnerability
5. Good listener
6. Non-judgmental
7. Fun
8. Supportive
9. Empathetic
10. Confident

THIRTEEN

DI and Dating

I was in middle school when I met my first love, "Ramon." Our story wasn't a love at first sight type of thing. I was about 12 years old when I kept hearing about this Puerto Rican charmer who had a different girl on his arm every week. He was the hot topic for most girls in my 7th grade class. Before we even met, I had heard about his cute Superman curl that fell on his forehead amongst his thick, dark brown locks.

"All the girls love him," my best friends Jessica and Michele would tell me. They had been in classes with Ramon before.

"He can't be that special," I would say in doubt. Part of my response was because I felt left out of the mix. The Needy Friend was rearing her head. I didn't want to lose my friends to some new kid who was charming my besties, especially since he was a boy!

"He even speaks Spanish," Michele said. "I heard him talking to his sister once when she came to get him from school." The fact that he was bilingual made him even more impressive to everyone, I'm sure of it.

Ramon seemed like he could relate to anyone; he was code-switching before we knew what it was. He came from a neighborhood with a lot of Mexican and Black families, not too far from where I grew up. He would play ball with the kids from that 'hood, yet, he could also hang out with upper-class white kids. He was a class clown, but got along with the teachers because he was smooth enough to talk his way out of trouble. Ramon was an anomaly in that he was a code-switching chameleon AND one of the smart kids. We both were enrolled in our school's magnet program, but we took our honors classes at different times. After hearing about him through my friends and seeing him only in passing, I finally had the chance to meet the famous Ramon during our magnet program's annual trip.

The field trip was in Colonial Williamsburg. We had a great time touring the area and learning how things were in the olden days. I was focused on the research, but you better believe I was also there to see what Ramon was all about. I was pleasantly surprised. He was funny and compassionate. We were at one of the houses on a tour and Michele fell pretty hard. I laughed. I couldn't help that I enjoy physical comedy! Although she was ok, he shot me a pretty judgy look for laughing at my friend. He also made sure to check on her throughout the rest of the trip. At that point, I realized he had his own relationship with her, having been in her class an entire year before.

I carried on. I was also thinking about another boy from a different school who was on the trip. He was a welcomed distraction from the anxiety I felt rising from the Needy

Friend narrative. When we returned from the field study, Ramon and I were on speaking terms. He learned that being friends with Jessica and Michele meant being friends with me too. I started giving him advice about what he should do about certain girls. I even noticed more girls throughout the rest of middle school were becoming my friends to get close to him. My social capital was increasing, and so was my fondness for Ramon.

By 9th grade, we were in a solid clique. Things were becoming more familiar and comfortable, except, the more I got to know Ramon, I realized I had developed feelings for him. For the life of me, I can't remember how these butterflies got in my stomach when he was around. Remember how I said my brother had shown me how a woman should be treated? I had found that in Ramon. It was the first time in my life I felt seen by a (non-related) boy. He was attentive and kind. He was talented and smart. And it helped that he had shot up a few inches on his journey into puberty. I was coming into my own as well. We started talking on the phone and leaning into our own private jokes. After a while, Jessica and Michele began working their magic to hook us up.

"He told me he likes you," Jessica told me. I had been freaking out about liking him so much, falling into the same trap as almost every girl I knew. I felt a little basic.

"Oh, really? Wow, that's cool," I said, downplaying my true feelings.

I was about 15 years old when Ramon and I made it official. The details escape me, but I'm pretty sure he played it cool when he asked me to "go togetha." Yeah, I didn't bring it up, I was too much of a chicken. Once it happened, we were in a natural stride. We had already formed a friendship, so we just called each other more.

On top of that, we were in marching band together, which takes up as much time as athletics. The marching band spent a lot of time together, like a family. Everyone knew Ramon and I were a thing. We were one of the many band couples on the scene. It was like being in some elite club: "The Taken Girls" at my high school. I had some trust issues here and there. I was the girl who pretty much knew all of Ramon's player secrets, the one who had given him advice all those times before. After a while, I ignored everything in me that said I would become another heart he broke. I didn't care. I needed something to fill the void I had at that time. Plus, I didn't have time to worry about what other girls lost. I needed to try grasping at examples of healthy relationships and focus on keeping mine. I needed to know how these things worked.

I watched Michele's parents, who are still married to this day. They had adopted me as their own, but I didn't live at my friend's house. The exposure wasn't enough to see how a healthy relationship functioned. I had to reference what I saw or didn't see in my own home. This made me angry. After sitting with my feelings, I can attest to the jealousy I had for Michele, having come from a two-parent household.

I was hurt that I had come from a broken home. There was embarrassment, and certainly a void. It's overwhelming to try to figure out things as a young person. I think this is why I was so desperate to hold on to Ramon; I wanted to make sure I locked down what I called a good thing. I didn't have hope that I would be worthy again. Not only was I completely boy crazy, but I was losing respect for my dad. I wondered why he wasn't fighting to be with my brother and me more so we could have our family back.

So here I was, working with what I had: Michele's parents' marriage as an example of optimism and anxiety, all in one. I tried to get some type of manly advice from Daddy. He and Mommy didn't stay married, but surely he at least had a do's and don'ts list. When he came over to check on my brother and me during Mommy's night shifts, I hinted at liking someone. I never said anything directly, but I would drop hints, curious about the type of advice I would get.

"Isn't that so sweet, how they look all in love?" We would be watching some sitcom where the lead characters were on a date or something.

"You know that's all fake. Things don't always go down like that," Daddy said. He's right. Love doesn't pan out in a perfect way, but I needed to hear that love was possible. Alas, it's so important to consider the source you take advice from.

I continued to test Daddy the older I got. I was curious about how he would react if I got my first boyfriend. The time never came for a sit-down conversation about how to engage in these relationships. It would have been great to hear some positive fatherly advice. My brother helped, though. He was quite popular with the ladies and so I could ask him for advice too.

"Don't seem too desperate," Alex told me once. Gee, thanks. Clearly, I was on my own to figure this thing out.

The chance finally came for me to introduce Ramon to my dad. There was no getting around it. I was about to turn 16 and Daddy arranged for me to treat a few friends to dinner and a movie. By then, Jessica and Michele had "serious" boyfriends too, so I wanted to have a triple date. There was no time like the present to tell him about my boyfriend.

"Daddy, so there's this guy. His name is Ramon. HeisinthebandandheisinALERTwithmesoheissmartandfunnyandAlexknowshimtoo," I said it all in one breath. Whew! I was nervous as hell.

"I need to meet him," Daddy demanded. That's a pretty common mandate from father to daughter. I was shocked it was so simple, almost too easy.

"My birthday party may be a good time," I said to him.

"OK. But he better come correct. You know I don't play dat," he said.

I was nervous. I think that's also pretty common when introducing your new man to your dad. I wanted to take this response as him protecting his little girl. I had been fantasizing about our relationship morphing into the "Daddy's Girl" dynamic, where he would be the doting father. I figured him leaving the house had meant he would be more involved since he wouldn't see us as much now. That didn't happen. With him gone, there was less opportunity for him to hear about the boy I liked. By inviting Ramon to my Sweet Sixteen, I had finally ripped off the bandaid.

I spent the weeks before my birthday dinner prepping my boyfriend for my dad. By then, Daddy had a reputation among my brother's friends and mine; they all knew not to mess with him. I don't think it helped Ramon. He kept talking about how nervous he was and asking me what to expect. I didn't have any new tips leading up to the birthday celebration. I didn't have much else to say beyond, "You know my dad is pretty tough."

The night of my Sweet Sixteen, we had dinner at a place that also had games and a bar. The owner allowed us to stay in place past the normal curfew for anyone under 21 years old. Ramon arrived, gave me my gift with a hug, and I walked him over to the section where my dad was hanging out.

"You got this. I promise it will be quick, he'll be leaving soon anyway," I coached.

The moment we had been preparing for was surprisingly...harmless. I introduced the two with a smile that said, 'don't you dare ruin my birthday.'

"Hey, I'm Ramon," my boyfriend said without his voice shaking.

"What's up, I'm Christian's dad."

"Nice to meet you," Ramon replied with a handshake.

"You too. So you're in the band?" Daddy asked.

This was going ok! Daddy made small talk the entire time, asking about the instrument Ramon played and his family. I felt good. It was something I was happy to witness; I still have a picture capturing this moment. Ramon could've pooped bricks, but he didn't let it show. I was even more impressed.

This moment meant a lot because Ramon symbolized a milestone for many reasons. After being made to feel like I couldn't do much good enough, I'd figured out how to get a boyfriend, keep him, and help him survive meeting my father. I had managed to show that I could be a respectable young lady with good grades AND a boyfriend. I could prove to my dad that love works and I knew what I was doing, that he could trust me. But most of all, I wasn't bringing my dad some random troublemaker, I had good judgment despite the fact that I questioned my ability to make healthy choices. I could gain my dad's approval by the people I chose to spend time with.

After a few laughs and pictures, my parents left me and my friends to our own devices. We were on our own to celebrate my birthday with pool, wings, and a trip to the movies to see the new Star Wars.

Being in a relationship was a huge adjustment. I had my two best friends to swap advice with about how and when to say things to make sure you keep your man. It helped, but how helpful could it have been coming from two other couples trying to figure it out. The truth was, I didn't have much to go by when it came to watching a healthy relationship. And I knew, thanks to my dad, that fairy tales don't exist.My conceptualization of relationships was based on two extremes: Disney's "True Love's Kiss" and utter despair. I was winging it under interesting circumstances.

Ramon and I were an interracial couple. To my knowledge, I was the first and only black girl he dated until then. I never was given the chance to meet his family. I saw them in passing, but he never introduced me as his girlfriend. To this day, I'm unsure whether he even told them who I was. Man, I must have looked like a groupie to his parents when I hung around. I was obviously more than that, but it wasn't made super clear. Later, I learned that Ramon was barely allowed to claim me.

"If we ever got married, what you think our kids' hair would look like?" I asked Ramon one night while we were on the phone. I was like many other young girls, living a fantasy.

"I don't know if that will happen," Ramon told me.

"You sound like you don't want that to happen," I said. I was obviously hurt.

"My mom always wanted me to marry a Puerto Rican girl," He said. There was hesitation in his voice. I knew he didn't want to hurt me. But I think it was his way of letting me know there was an expiration date on a love I thought would last forever.

My heart dropped as I ended the call. I thought I found something that would help solidify my self-esteem. I was happy to have found him. But this conversation changed everything. I was suddenly not good enough. It rang in my ears because it proved my dad right. Daddy checked in on our relationship from time to time. He didn't wince when I talked about him. But he did offer some advice about dating a boy who looked white.

"You be careful. You know how ignorant people can be," Daddy would tell me. I understand now, he was trying to teach me to be careful of the bigots in SC. In fact, he was right. When we went to the fair once, we got the ugliest stares for holding hands. Ramon dropped my hand a few times to avoid a potential confrontation.

I became more sensitive to Ramon's mom's judgment of me. She triggered me almost the same way my Dad did. She made me think that I wasn't good enough for her son. At home, Daddy made me feel like I wasn't good enough for him to stick around. Although Ramon's mom and my dad had different reasons, their actions activated the same sentiments. It seemed that nothing I did anywhere could keep an interest. Being in a relationship with Ramon meant I was performing for his mom, which is a lot for a teenage girl. On top of this, I was also competing with new girls who came to school or the next hot thing waiting in line to date my Ramon. I had every DI symptom screaming at me before I knew what it was. How stressful!

Eventually, I found myself giving in to things that went against how I was raised. I lost my virginity to Ramon at 15. It was completely consensual and I was really more excited than anything. We talked about it at length: strategies on how we would do it and how to avoid getting caught. It was nice to have him listen to my concerns. I didn't feel pressured. I certainly felt ready. I was super horny, yet another new emotion. Ramon told me over and over that I didn't have to go for it, and he meant it. He was fine hanging out. But I wanted to use something I knew would work to keep a boy interested: my body. This desperation stemmed from the same void I knew Ramon was filling for me. It didn't matter that I didn't really know what I was doing.

The main guidance my parents gave on sex was a book they made my brother and I read in fourth grade about how babies were made. My mom also talked to me about her own struggles and what not to do. In discussions of sex, many parents make the mistake of leaving out the details of how positive sex can be. Shame is usually the center of this conversation, instead of how sex is a gift that a person needs to be ready to give and receive. The messages I received were that only a "fast" girl has sex as a teenager and that she will have increased likelihood of becoming pregnant or catching a sexually transmitted infection.

With my father's negative judgment about everything else, I could imagine what he would say if he knew I was even holding hands with Ramon! There was a conflict regarding whether I should employ my plan to keep my boyfriend by any means or try to make my father proud by being a good girl. When Ramon and I finally did have sex, I had so many questions. I felt ashamed, proud, embarrassed, hopeful, accomplished, confused and overwhelmed.

One thing I didn't feel was empowered. I didn't feel comfortable to be inquisitive with my dad about many things. The select few topics of discussion were business only: school and basic needs. I couldn't begin a conversation about sex. Now, you may be thinking, *Girl, I would never tell my dad about that either!* I get it. But a healthy relationship with open communication with a father or father figure would help unlock that fear. It's totally possible to have heavy conversations with the right level of trust safety. I could talk to my mother. She and I had a special bond but, at the time, I knew she reported things to my dad. It was their co-parenting strategy, no matter how estranged we all were. I was too nervous that my budding sex life would get back to Daddy to entrust her.

Not too long later, Ramon and I broke up. I remember the emotional conversation we had.

"But why? I can't just be your friend," I cried.

"I just want to go back to the way things used to be," Ramon told me. "I don't want to lose you...as a friend."

"I just don't see my life without you," I pleaded. Man, my world was crumbling fast. That's what happens when you don't have an anchor, a solid secure sense of yourself.

The weeks after our breakup were hard. Here came a stream of heifers going after my man. Watching him move on to the next was even harder. I had to sit there and see him laugh with another girl, a girl from the color guard in the very band where we played together! I was able to move on a little myself by entertaining other boys. It was unfamiliar territory for a while, as I wasn't used to the attention I was getting. The more I healed from losing my relationship with Ramon, the more I realized how cute I was and that he wasn't the only one who would give me the time of day. It may have also helped that people knew I had given up my virginity, as I was now a girl who wasn't afraid to offer her body. I had found the voice I lost over the years until then. My ability to control what I gave to the boys who swarmed became my new voice. This was a new habit I learned that would take me through my college years as well, a very hard lesson to unlearn.

In the midst of all this, I was dealing with the impending doom of the serious relationship my dad was building with a woman who wasn't my mother. I was in high school when I learned about her. It was very subtle really, I barely noticed the signs at first.

My brother and I kept getting clothes from my dad. Suddenly, he was providing for us in a very tangible, trackable way that I appreciated. I had a job by then, but it was icing on the cake that I could save some of my paycheck and get free, stylish duds from Old Navy. Daddy kept bringing home bags of clothes because the store always had killer sales.

"Wow! Thanks. These are cute. I'm glad you know what I like," I told Daddy. I was almost surprised at his taste for a teenage girl.

"Oh, no problem. I have one of my friends shop for me. She's nice enough to pick up what she can find on sale," Daddy replied.

This friend was becoming a fixture around Daddy's family. Apparently, everyone except for me knew she was more than a friend. My paternal grandmother's beauty shop was the place to be for me on weekends. I ran into her sitting in Grandma's chair, getting her hair curled. She was about five years older than me, which is way younger than my dad.

"Thanks for the clothes! I really like them," I told Telee. I looked her in the face and smiled, not picking up on any of the energy around me.

"Oh! You're welcome," Telee said kindly.

One day, I got confirmation. I didn't have a ride to my job after school that particular afternoon. Mommy was at work, so I rang Daddy.

"Oh, you good. I'll send Telee to get you," Daddy told me. I thanked him. One thing I learned from him was punctuality. It's a pet peeve of mine to be late. Plus, I was getting paid for every minute I was on the clock.

When Telee pulled up, she was driving my dad's white Mercedes. The stick shift he never had the patience to teach me to drive. This was Strike One. It hit me: Telee is serious. I was livid. *She's not my mom. Who is she to him? Am I tripping? How does she have Daddy's car? What is really going on? Nah, this can't be it. Wait until I tell Alex! How could I miss this?!*

Not long after that, they moved in together. Strike Two. My dad told me it was because he was saving her from a dangerous neighborhood. All I knew was, he didn't let my brother and me spend the night in his tiny apartment. It didn't make sense that he was moving Telee into the area he lived in, which wasn't much better than her old place. At any rate, I believed he thought he was protecting my brother and me. But it felt like abandonment. It certainly didn't fit my picture of how a daughter should be treated. I learned yet another lesson here: new relationships don't have to regard the people adjacent to it and therefore, can be destructive. They can even cost you the ones you love. Our family unit was broken for good when Daddy began nurturing the new relationship.

Mommy fell on hard times and could barely pay the bills. Eventually we lost our apartment and had to move somewhere cheaper. *How could Daddy be making time for another woman when I was living with my mother in a hotel and my brother was living with his friend?* I felt betrayed and disrespected. Years later, I learned that there was some mismanagement of finances--my mother wasn't the best at handling money. At any rate, this was an embarrassing introduction, that Telee had to see me basically homeless. In addition, it was infuriating that she had been around family who never said anything to me about her. I felt entitled to the information. I was flat-out jealous.

If my dad couldn't sit me down to talk about his dating life, how could I learn to manage my own? Here was yet another opportunity to teach me how to properly enter a relationship, with no secrets or shame. My parents were not legally divorced until after I met Telee. I immediately lost respect for this woman and still struggle with it today. This also gave me insight about the standards I would later keep with my future suitors. There are many parts of this story that hurt me. What stands out the most is the memory of my father defending Telee many times over me, when I finally did voice my opinion about their relationship.

I was at the shop once, getting my regular relaxer from my grandmother. Telee and my dad had been together for a few years now, as I was off to college. My worst nightmare was coming to pass: they were getting married. Strike Three. They'd been living together for years by now and Telee invited me to be in the wedding as a formality, I presume. I had no real relationship with her. Grandma asked me what I thought about it.

"I'm not sure I want to be part of it. I will go, I guess," I told Grandma. By that time, Daddy and I were on the outs; our relationship was rocky.

"Oh, why you say that, Christian," Grandma asked me. I assumed she wanted to really help me through what was obviously an emotional time. I told her how hurt I was that this wedding meant my parents were really over. I was sad and mad all at once. I was nervous about what this meant for me. Telee had already replaced me in a lot of ways: Daddy taught HER to drive. Daddy let HER spend the night and have the time I was supposed to get. Daddy was building a new bond with HER family. Add in the age factor and how could I not feel replaced?

I poured my heart out to Grandma. Later that day, my phone rang. It was Daddy, yelling in my ear that I needed to stop talking junk about Telee and that I didn't know how much she had done for my brother and me. It was devastating. He had not heard any of the message. It was like a bad game of telephone; I don't know what exactly got relayed. He had taken Grandma's word for it without asking how I was or what I thought. I wanted to tell him he was doing a horrible job balancing my needs as well as his fiancé's, that he had dropped the ball with my brother too. It was like he wanted to erase us and start over. But he didn't give me the chance.

"You're disrespectful. I didn't raise you like that!" Daddy yelled. "You hurt Telee and she didn't ask for any of this," he added. It was as if he didn't care to appease me. He seemed to want to fix his relationship with Telee at my expense.

"Do you hear yourself? I can't even get a word in," I said before I hung up. He called back a few times and started yelling as soon as I answered. I hung up every time after that.

I could have witnessed a great example of how a courtship is performed. Daddy and Telee would have been hard to accept either way, but it was a chance for him to show me from the beginning how a woman should be treated. Instead, I learned betrayal. I knew jealousy and doubt watching my dad and his new wife. The messages I took from my dad about dating only increased my insecurities about myself.

Like a good daughter, I went to the wedding. I declined taking part in the ceremony, but I wore her favorite color: purple. I smiled. I waved. I danced. Again, I was in a position where I had to perform to keep someone's attention. And if I'm honest, I wanted my dad's attention even during that entire whirlwind of his wedding. I wanted him to be proud. I needed it. But I had been replaced. My voice didn't matter. He had moved on, like most of the men I dated. Thankfully, I had my own car by then. My brother and I were out by the time the cake was served.

The first official date I had when I got to undergrad was with a dude named Albert. There was a dance to kick off freshman year, hosted by one of the most popular fraternities on campus. Albert was a member. We had been preparing for weeks for a charity fashion show sponsored by the frat and I had gotten to know him during that time. One day, he asked me to dinner.

"You know, we can go to the party together. But let's grab food first," he said.

"You mean us?" I was confused. I had never been asked out on a date straight-forwardly like that.

"Yeah," Albert laughed. "You and me. I'll take you to dinner then you can meet up with your friends afterward."

I politely accepted the invitation.

We ended up having a great time at a really cute restaurant. I was totally rusty on date small talk with a cute boy--well, man--but we made it work. Once we got going, it was pretty easy to tell him how my freshman year was going and how excited I was for one of my first college parties. That was it. We got back to campus and said goodbye after he made sure I was good and connected with my friends. No kiss. No sex. Just good company.

This was probably one of the most memorable times in college because it was so rare. I had to wait a few years for my next "no-obligation" date, which was with my now-husband. He took me out all the time. Looking back, I am torn between feeling regretful for not dating as much or just plain relieved that I didn't. I didn't believe I was dating material given what I witnessed growing up; I wondered whether that had ruined me.

So, what's dating material? You know, the nice girl who deserves a special courtship because she lived her life "right." At least, that's what I told myself at the time. I truly believed that after all I had done to defy the lessons instilled in me, I would be living that karma forever. I would never get a dream man and I would pay for it with my body until I died. Hope. It was one thing I didn't have after being left so emotionally raw by my father.

I was a miserable, self-hating, confused person. I carried all this into relationships. The better term would be *situationships*, as I didn't get very far into dating. There was sex. That was it. I didn't know how to navigate a relationship and was tired of trying to figure it out. I had already been plagued by the loss of a crucial relationship already, the one with my dad. Dating with DI was an eye opener for me. Of course, it takes a while to redirect if you're afraid of positive change like I was for a long time.

At this point in my life when I spiraled. My DI was in full effect. For three years, my dad and I had not spoken a word. I questioned my worth because I felt abandoned. The way I saw it, he 'had a new life with his wife. Every birthday, Father's Day, and major holiday that passed was harder than it should have been. Now that I think of it, they were days filled with resentment>>excessive alcohol use>>sex>>crying. All the feels came up. All the thoughts surrounding my worth were brought forward. I felt inadequate and found it hard to make healthy decisions. I wondered how my boyfriend could possibly want to stay in a relationship with me. I began intentionally sabotaging my relationship because I was good at destroying things instead of trying to fix them. This part was easy, as I had mostly watched the demise of relationships instead of their healthy construction and ongoing maintenance. Unfortunately the ones that stuck out were the painful downfalls. At points when my husband and I were dating and supposed to be faithful, I flirted with other men, no doubt looking for the attention I desperately craved. It didn't matter that I had found something fulfilling. I couldn't get myself to a place to receive the love because the truth is, I didn't recognize it. I guess I thought I did because I watched Disney movies my entire life. It was the majority of what I had to go by, and it just wasn't enough.

Many times, I meet clients who ask me if what they're feeling is normal...*Christian, am I crazy?* I always rebut with validation that they're responding normally to an abnormal event. It's my go-to response, I even have to tell it myself. The roller coaster I was on with my dad was in a twisted reality where I experienced trauma bonding.

This is a concept that says we find ways to survive traumatic events (no matter how big or small) that involve someone we are supposed to love and be loved by. This could look like wanting to return to them after they hurt us physically or emotionally. It could mean we seek approval despite experiencing negative judgement from the person bringing the pain. People who experience trauma bonding may cook and clean because they are answering the innate desire for connection with someone, even if they hurt us. It's a way to be seen no matter the expense paid.

We are wired for belonging and interaction, which can skew our view of relationships. It is what drives the idea that we must settle for less than we are worthy of. This trauma bonding behavior is born out of confusion; our brains are answering our needs, but there is not always a filter to address the resulting negative emotions. Many people associate this concept with survivors of Intimate Partner Violence (IPV). It is what traditionally makes it difficult to leave harmful relationships. Emotional traumas, the residue that is negative, overwhelming feelings that take a toll on us for a while after the events, definitely take work to heal from. You need to know it's possible to be redeemed. It is freeing. We all deserve it. There is a light at the end of the tunnel.

FOURTEEN

Self-Care Check-in

1. How have the messages you learned from your father impacted your choices in partners?
2. What have you noticed about your DI symptoms in your dating life? Was there a time they were more prevalent than others? What do you think made them fluctuate?
3. What did you learn about yourself from specific dating relationships? How do you think you have evolved or been stunted in these areas?

Activity:

Before becoming intimate with a partner, it's important to know yourself. By now, you've hopefully learned more about yourself. I wonder if you have taken time to really be...just you. This exercise will help you become more in tune with what your partner may notice when you experience certain things. But it's helpful if you notice them first and make proper adjustments.

Look into a mirror. Give yourself at least five minutes to stare at your reflection. Get to know your features when you think positive thoughts and feel positive emotions, as well as negative ones. How does your face change? Do a quick body scan and focus on the sensations of your body from head to toe. Get in tune with how you respond to certain thoughts, memories, feelings.

If you notice any negativity, ask yourself what you need and see the self-care list for ideas. Be empowered to make the change and fulfill your needs yourself. If you're a spiritual person, meditate on the needs, breathe, and attract what you know will help. Do the work to elevate self-awareness. That way, whatever your partner adds is icing on the cake!

FIFTEEN

DI and Marriage

June 11, 2016 was the best day of my life. It was my wedding day. People judge me for marking this day as THE best day ever because our son was already 5 years old by then. Even after our amazing little boy took his first steps, was finally potty trained and doing well in kindergarten, I stand by the fact that my wedding day is my favorite of all. I'd kissed so many frogs by then with little to no hope of having a husband one day. I was battling with insecurities that hindered progress and potentially decent relationships. But oh! I found the man I wanted to be with forever. I was so happy! And now, I reached the day my life would change; I was going to be a wife.

"It is finally herrreeeeee," Michele sang to me on June 11, 2016. She and my other close friends were coming over to get their makeup done.

"I know! I can't even believe it...I'm so calm too," I replied. I'd spent the morning fantasizing about how Tony would look at me when I walked down the aisle. I knew he would be so sexy in his suit.

"It's a good sign you're so at peace," Michele said. "It means you know what you want. You guys are finally in a good place and on the same page. You're going to be a wife!"

By then, all my close friends except one were married. I struggled with being the only legally single person in the group, especially since Tony and I had dated for so much longer than everyone else. We were getting married on our 10th year dating anniversary.

"Remember when we broke up that one time and I drove down I-77 crying and looking for a cliff to drive off? Man, I was crazy," I said to my friend Crystal.

"Girl, I'm just glad you called me. I couldn't understand nothing you were saying: 'Tony.' 'I can't.' 'Overrrrrr,'" Crystal joked. We could laugh about it then, but she was describing one of the most devastating times in my relationship with Tony. He'd told me he didn't want to be with me anymore after finding out that I entertained someone else during our long-distance relationship.

"I was so worried. It wasn't even the last time we broke up," I said to my girls while we drank wine and giggled at all the tea that was the 'Christian and Tony Saga.'

My wedding day was a metaphor for many things: *Security*, because I was sure being married to the man I loved would only strengthen our family's foundation; *Safety*, because I always felt he protected me emotionally and physically; *Acceptance*, because he saw me...like really saw me and stayed. I felt extremely blessed that he still wanted me, and that I had learned to accept myself through his reinforcement.

It took a long time for me to realize that I don't need anyone else to complete me. Society conditions us to believe we need other people to be whole, rather than the fact that we can be whole on our own, having done our work to build our spiritual, emotional, and physical wealth. Those of us with DI symptoms have an interesting journey to being holistically whole. There are messages we have to undo. Things we have to unsee. Appropriate blame to set and rational responsibilities to take on.

When we enter serious relationships, especially intimate ones, it can bring out the little girl who learned insecurity from dealing with her father. We flounder, trying to hold onto the goodness we feel. These interactions bring forward things about ourselves we thought we buried deeply. Nurturing a close relationship means holding up a mirror to our ugliness and pulling out the microscope, which makes sure no traumas are left behind!

Tony and I met at Rio's Nightlife on Main Street in my hometown. I was with Michele and a few other friends on spring break my sophomore year. I was wearing a really cute vest over a glittery tank top, jeans, and a long string of pearls. I saw him from across the room in a colorful Lacrosse shirt. As the night went on, Michele and I made our rounds until we were close enough for him to motion me over for a dance. I dropped it like it was hot, showing him my best moves. When the song was over I turned around.

"What's your name?" He asked me.

"Christian!" I yelled over the music.

He grabbed his phone, signifying that he wanted my number. I gave it to him right away. His smile is what captured me and keeps me swooning today.

"You want to come back and chill at my house?" Tony asked me.

"You can just call me tomorrow," I replied. Unbeknownst to me, I had passed a test.

Tony later revealed he was trying to see what kind of girl I was: good girl or the hot, fast one. Thankfully, I felt the need to do something different that night.

The next day was the big St. Patrick's Day Parade in our town. Tony called me to follow up about a date. Yes, this was another rare time a man asked me out. I was giddy. Part of me knew it was something special. The other part was just. Plain. Nervous!

I had already been in full-blown DI mode. I was questioning my self-worth, wondering if I could be enticing enough to keep the conversation going. *What will I talk about with an older man? What should I wear? How do you act around a guy in a restaurant?* I wasn't well-versed in dating etiquette. The stories I made up in my head were nuts.

The night finally came. Tony took me to an Applebee's near his apartment. I sat there humming songs that played over our heads and trying to avoid eye contact.

"You're going to sing every song that comes on, huh?" Tony finally said.

"I just love music! This is my jam," I joked. I wasn't sure what else to do but sing, act cute, and be funny.

The rest of the date went pretty decent. We went back to his apartment afterwards and watched TV. And there was no sex! This was also something new about us. Tony didn't make me feel like I had to give up anything. I wasn't compelled to put on a show for him.

We communicated regularly the rest of that year before school ended and at the close of the semester I came home straight to him. We were inseparable all summer 2006, riding out to our soundtrack, Pharrell's *In My Mind* album. Every single day was spent together. If I wasn't at work, I was with Tony. If Tony wasn't at work, he was on his way to me. We spoke during his lunch breaks every day and I met him at his apartment when he got off the same time every night. We were so into each other I barely saw my best friends that summer. They eventually got on me about that.

"Um, we don't know this man," Afton told me. She was only half joking about the possibility of me ending up in a ditch someplace.

"When can we meet him?" Michele asked.

This led to one of the most awkward dinners ever. I arranged for my two besties and Tony to meet at a bar for wings one night. We talked about the weather, sports, and other things people have on the agenda when you're forced to get to know one another. I didn't care. I knew I was in this relationship for the long haul and it would require he got to know my life. I thought it was sweet my friends were worried about me and even sweeter Tony, my introverted man, humored me. This was just the beginning of our courtship. He was slowly breaking down the walls I had built. He was showing me the possibility of having it all without having to give it all up.

Our first summer together was coming to a close and it was time for me to return to college. It was mostly a bitter moment, but sweet that he was expressing how much he would miss me. I learned it was ok to accept that type of attention now that I was getting it regularly. Every day we spent together revealed a part of Tony I knew I wanted to be a witness to forever. I was thankful to have experienced such unconditional grace from a man, especially when I didn't know if it would ever come or how to handle it after everything I watched in my parents' relationship.

One day, I got a call from the controller's office at my school. My mom had fallen behind on tuition payments for the upcoming semester. Although I had a good thing with Tony, it was hard to tell him about the issues I was having. I tried and failed to hide it from him.

"What's wrong with you?" Tony asked me when I got off the phone.

"I don't think I can go back to school. We don't have the money," I cried. It was devastating. Without financial assistance from my dad, I couldn't cover the bills. I was embarrassed about having to let Tony know about yet another failure from my relationship with Daddy. Plus, I was mad at my father all over again.

"How much is it?" Tony was getting out his phone to check his bank account. I immediately stopped crying.

"$800," I said slowly. I wasn't sure what to think. But the last thing on my mind was what he would say next.

"Let me know how and when to send the money. I got you," He replied. That was it. I was floored. No one had ever done something like this for me, at least not overtly. It was when I fell in love for real.

Paying my tuition wouldn't be the last time I felt supported by Tony. The rest of my college days meant I had him to help me buy books, pay my rent when I came up short, make sure I had groceries and gas. It was amazing to have someone take care of me like that. I began to learn to accept the help. He was my person and it felt good. He took on responsibilities most of my friends' parents were filling for them. My mother did her best, but Tony filled in gaps she couldn't. Like a father.

Since the beginning of our relationship, he symbolized stability. Tony's and my blooming happened at a time when my relationship with my dad was dying. I became more dependent on Tony than ever to fill the void. I'm quite sure this is where the pressure was on for him. But he handled it with grace. He was helping me to undo the anxiety I learned from the home I grew up in. He balanced me out and became the person I could go to when I was unravelling. I was sure I wanted to stay around forever.

I thought of all of this as I sat there with my girls two hours before my wedding. Tony and I had come so far. It was finally time. Ironically, Daddy walked me down the aisle toward the man he swore would leave me. I wanted him to be part of the day because we were in the midst of trying to repair our relationship for the five years prior when my son was born. I remember crying with my dad before we took the long walk toward Tony. We had prayed together and laughed. He seemed to be proud of me and love me that day. Despite the fact that we were talking again, we were both sweeping so much under the rug. We hadn't worked through the real issues that drove us apart. I had only slightly forgiven him, for the sake of the concept of family. I told myself I didn't have time for the drama and it would work itself out. This is a sneaky symptom of DI: the avoidance piece. This mechanism in our brain is there to protect us. We would rather "deal with it later" than address things head on. I was in that mode. I wanted to focus on my literally growing family. On my wedding day, I was wrapping up my first trimester for baby Number Two. Instead of taking steps back, I was looking forward to the next chapter.

--

Funny thing about marriage is you take your old you with you if you're not careful.

There was a part of me that married my husband because I was still trying to prove to my father that I could make something work that he couldn't. That I could still be loved when he didn't think Tony would stay with me. And that the man I was marrying was more than a suitable replacement for my dad and the things he couldn't and/or wouldn't do for me. In fact, it was a step up! Call me the Petty Queen, but these are real, valid thoughts and feelings that informed the victory I felt on my wedding day and well into the first year of our marriage.

Since Tony and I were cohabitating for at least 5 years prior to getting married, I was determined to make a distinction between the boyfriend/girlfriend dynamic. I also saw this as an opportunity to rid myself of the childish ways of my 20s. Turns out marriage is not a magic wand; those ways are still melting away. All my insecurities were heightened. It was as if I was becoming even more sensitive to subtle changes as days charged on. I started realizing how much being with my husband poked at my DI symptoms. For example, if I made a new recipe that was a little iffy to begin with, my husband wasn't afraid to tell me.

"There's something on the chicken," Tony might say. He has a special way of expressing his thoughts.

"WHAT YOU MEAN?! I'M TRYING SOMETHING NEW. I'M TRYING TO BE A GOOD WIFE, I'VE WORKED ALL---" I'd scream.

"Yo, chill, Christian," Tony would reply. "I'm just asking a question. I can't ask you a question without you trippin all the time."

My irritability reared its head often. If Tony didn't like something I did, I made up stories in my head: *He's going to leave me if I don't make this right. I just keep messing up. This is too hard. How can I be a wife and a mother? This is overwhelming. I keep meaning to go to the gym, but I can't make the time. My body is changing after the babies. They say you have to do what you did to get him in order to keep him.*

The story I make up in my head is that I'm a terrible wife and he is going to leave me because of these mistakes. I only heard the critical tone of my father instead of my husband literally telling me to lay off the salt. It's possible the man just didn't want to develop major health problems at my hand. If I put on makeup or do my hair differently, I expect to hear how amazing I look within three minutes of applying the finishing touches. Anything outside this...interesting standard may cause a spiral where I'm telling myself I must not be good enough to attract my own husband's attention.

So far, I sound pretty needy. I'm going to own that. I have to know where I'm starting before I can make any adjustments, right? Gary Chapman, author of *The 5 Love Languages: The Secret to Love that Lasts*, would say that my top love language is Words of Affirmation. I experience love the strongest when someone tells me affirming, complimentary things. This love language theory gained traction because of its simple formula to conceptualize how to communicate/receive not only love, but approval. I believe that those of us who have moderate to severe DI try to compensate for the lack of affirmation and/or approval we received in our childhood.

From the beginning of my courtship with my husband I sought his approval, just like with any other man I dated. When I made our first meal as husband and wife, I sought his approval for how healthy and tasty it was. When I made mistakes, the arguments were almost always worse because no matter how wrong I was, I wanted him to approve of my thoughts. It was a stressful place to be, my head. I developed plotlines where I starred as the insecure heroine. It looked a little like this:

FADE IN

LIVING ROOM. QUIET FALL EVENING

The children are laid to bed for the night. There are toys on the floor of the living room. The house still smells of the crockpot meal the family had for dinner that evening: beef stew. Pan over to Chrisitan and Tony, who are stretched on the couch, each on their own devices.

CHRISTIAN

So, Babe. Let me tell you about this crazy thing that
happened at work...

Before she can start her story, Tony raises his hands to give the "time out" signal.

TONY

Wait a minute. Can I ask you a question?

He pauses. Then moves on when given the hesitant, affirmative nod from his wife.

TONY

Why you ain't clean the shower door or windows? I mean, I ain't said nothing all this time...

CHRISTIAN

What does it matter?! You always picking on me for the little things and you don't notice the things I do around here that are so much more important!! I'm done! You will not make me feel like I've done nothing when I take care of your kids! I'm not finna sit here and take this---

TONY

I AM NOT YOUR DADDY, CHRISTIAN!!

Silence fills the room as the last statement lingers. Christian starts to cry and leaves the scene. Tony looks after her, with his chest heaving and his head shaking. Suddenly, Christian storms back into the room, crying and shaking herself.

CHRISTIAN

I can't believe you would say that! What does it have to do with me telling you that you always make me feel like I don't do enough?! I work hard, Tony. You're not going to take over like you're the perfect husband. Because you're not. When's the last time you cut the grass? Huh? I'm sick of telling you I have allergies and that's why I'm not doing it!

Pan to Tony. Who simply stares at Christian as she rattles on about what she is doing right and what he is doing wrong. This continues for about five minutes, until Christian is finally fed up that Tony hasn't responded (although she hasn't let him) and officially retires to their bedroom, without telling her husband about the crazy thing that happened at work that day.

This particular evening was one for the books. It was the night I finally received an objective point of view about my reactions during a disagreement. I thought about this night many times after that. Could it be that my defenses were so tough that I didn't let my husband in? Was I so driven by the fear of being made a fool of in my marriage that I only responded harshly to criticism instead of receiving it with love? Yes. The answer was yes. My self-preservation instincts kicked in when I sensed my security was threatened, and I panicked and went into fight or flight mode; my go-to reaction being "fight".

Recall that survivors of overwhelming adverse mental, emotional, physical, and spiritual events survived because of the way brains are conditioned. We are wired for survival mode, where we respond to actual or perceived threats in certain ways. When we find a reaction we like the most, we stick to it, no matter how irrational it is. For example, if a bear [threat] approaches we will either square up [fight] or run [flight]. There's also a tendency to freeze, where our body thinks it best to stay put with no reaction at all. This is how the human species is still here; it's always been the survival of the fittest. Whether we experienced a "typical" traumatic event is not a requirement for us to have learned certain ways to interact in our environments. All our "bears" are different.

Brene Brown, the shame researcher and absolute genius in the field of mental health, describes shame shields. This concept also applies to my response when threatened. If we maintain Brown's definition that shame means "I am bad," it hurts sometimes when people really see you. Thus, we respond in a way to protect us. Brown submits that we use shame shields: we move away [flight] by withdrawing from that which makes us feel shameful. Moving toward, where we force ourselves into the space [fight]. This lean in may be more harmful. We also move against [fight, again] where we misplace blame and argue.

The arguments I had during the time I was actually getting along with my dad again were... special. I was dealing with pent-up frustration that he hadn't apologized or validated me. I took it out on my husband. Whenever I was possibly wrong, my shame spiral, as Brown calls it, took off. I felt seen, and not in a good way. I damn near had flashbacks of my dad berating my mother, thereby activating my determination to speak up for myself and make sure I was heard. It didn't matter as much that I hurt my husband. I had responses ready and sometimes I stored away lethal quips to avoid the emotional pain at all cost. I walked around with a chip on my shoulder in the place that was supposed to be safe: My home. My marriage.

My behaviors were clearly learned. Not having stellar examples of decent conflict resolution strengthened with every word from my boyfriend. He saw my shame. I was exposed as an emotionally immature little girl who didn't know what love was. A girl who felt worthless, confused, and insecure. I would rather argue him down then feel those things. Another funny thing, the more I pushed, the worse it got. There was barely a resolution. I supposed one unresolved issue begets another unresolved issue and so on.

It's so interesting how our younger selves enter the room when we are threatened. I can't help but think that's who my parents regressed to as they argued. It was indeed like watching two children fight. My disagreements with my husband, no matter how large or small, also activated the fight in me to an extreme degree. It was overwhelming because of the spiral of thoughts swirling in my head. *Is he saying I'm dumb because I didn't pay attention to this point? Is he going to leave me? It's not ok for him to raise his voice AND disagree. Be petty. He's going to see right through your small mindedness, anyway. Don't back down like your mother did.*

It's so toxic. Complicating this narrative was the fact that I didn't have the skill set to effectively articulate my points, nor did my pride allow me to say when I was wrong. I thought that if I admitted defeat I would just be racking up marbles in the "reasons-for-him-to-leave-you" jar. This jar, when full, would give my husband all the ammo needed to walk out because he will have taken way more negativity than he deserved.

Oftentimes, as life partners, we want to make the other party happy. It's what reinforces our purpose and adds to what we hope to be a healthy relationship. For women with DI, it's a bit more complicated. There's the sense of obligation to our partners when we are insecurely attached. Recall the characteristics of anxious and anxious-fearful attachment, where the person is afraid their partner will leave them. In a marital relationship, there is the tendency to engage in behaviors for the sole purpose of keeping the relationship together. Making a good meal or doing the laundry may not come out of love but paranoia of abandonment. Any threat to the quality of the work can throw off the status quo, like it did in my case sometimes.

For the securely attached woman with DI, there's the possibility of the independent woman who doesn't appear to need anything. Perhaps, she has it all together with her career and/or responsibilities with her husband. She even manages to keep things in tact with her partner and their children! Man, this can look like a picture-perfect situation. I treated a woman who presented with these issues in her marriage.

"I don't know why he doesn't understand me," Toni said, confused. "I cook, clean, manage our finances! It seems like he doesn't appreciate me," she shared.

"I wonder what his place is in your marriage. Talk about how you express your vulnerability to him," I prodded.

It was important that Toni understood she had a habit of making her husband feel unnecessary. She loved him, it was what brought her to therapy. She wanted to know how she was contributing to the recent arguments and ominous vibe. But she overlooked that her definition of security didn't involve other people. She didn't see that her idea of strength meant she neglected her own needs, hence the lack of support she felt.

"Daddy told me I was strong. And I always knew I was by watching the way he moved. He let me know I was beautiful, smart, and that anyone would be lucky to be my friend or my lover," Toni shared.

We talked more about the delicate balance of relationships. That she didn't need to take on all her cares alone. We explored her scripts, the messages she took away from those conversations with her father. She was able to take a closer look at the things she learned from him. Although she gained a sense of empowerment, one that is helpful for all of us, she missed the context for the information. In her father's case, the context was inspired by pain. He was protecting himself from being slighted the way he had been treated in his life. So he learned to do everything on his own. It was a true testament to how one generation impacts the marriage of another; talk about family of origin impact.

As soon as Tony finally told me "I'm not your dad," I knew it was time to make changes. I say "finally" because there were many times he kept his opinions about my responses to him locked up. He eventually admitted that he felt like he couldn't ask me anything because I acted so defensively when asked to do him a favor or change something around. I wanted to control everything and it was obvious. My hang ups about doing everything right was coming from a place of competing with my dad, again, showing him I could make something work he couldn't. My control was also a product of wanting to prove him wrong. It was so overbearing to my husband that he adopted an "eff it" attitude, something he thought would be safer to enforce than arguing me down all the time. That's not a way to live. It's not the relationship I wanted. But there I was, contributing to what could have been the demise of the marriage I was working so hard to keep together to spite my father.

I so love that my husband could identify my DI without me even telling him what I was dealing with. I hadn't realized it or admitted my DI to myself up to that point. Doing so would mean I was weak. It meant I had potential to be the lonely woman my dad thought I would be for whatever reason. I was living in the space of insecurity and revenge. There were times that I found myself listening to respond to Tony instead of to understand him. My goal was to be perceived as correct and strong, so I wouldn't look stupid for not knowing things. I didn't care that it was at the expense of our relationship. I just remember wanting to be the opposite of what my mother showed me when she argued with Daddy. I wanted to stand my ground against the objections Tony presented. It got to the point where I didn't fully believe Tony should have an opinion about anything. I had a sharp tongue that I used as a weapon to feel power instead of pain--I was turning into my dad. When I realized I was hearing his logic and his tone issue from my body, I entered therapy immediately.

Kim. Oh, what an angel. She is truly a Godsend of a therapist because she helped me see the flaw in my thinking. I was so sure that keeping my defenses up would help protect me from the inevitable pain Tony would inflict. It's overwhelming to think that I had to be responsible for all my feelings. I had never considered how toxic my logic was; I truly believed after years of being with Tony that I had to protect myself. I always felt safe, but emotional pain is different. I knew I needed to keep him out of that bubble for my own good.

"It's hard to accept that you have surpassed your father spiritually and emotionally. On a developmental level, you've matured past him," Kim told me one day. I had just finished reading her a letter to my father. She had assigned me that one thing clients dread: to write a letter to the person who hurt you. It took me a while to write it. I procrastinated all the way up to the night before my session.

"I know. I'm so disappointed and surprised. I held Daddy up on a pedestal, even after all he put me through," I told her.

Since my father and I were on speaking terms, I wanted to hold on to the fantasy I had of being a Daddy's Girl. Leading up to and after the wedding, I leaned on him for the advice I'd wanted during the years I didn't have him around. It was like I was trying to make up for lost time. His advice influenced my interactions with my husband. This is a common occurrence for Daddy's Girls who become wives: They have a hard time determining who to listen to after they say "I do."

"You can't help that God is taking you somewhere different," Kim said.

I needed to process the impact of my dad's judgmental comments in my head while I made decisions about my husband. It was hard to separate. Plus, I needed to discuss my vision of my family with my husband, not my father. My dad wasn't even aware of the conversations I had in my head seeking his approval. I needed to redirect my energy into conversation with my Heavenly Father, instead of someone who stressed me out! I needed to begin to see myself the way God saw me, the way my husband did, and correct the narratives I had picked up as a child. I needed to see that it was ok to make mistakes and to trust that I will learn from them and be better.

I consider my marriage like a redo, to an extent. What better setting to practice taking and giving criticism in a loving way than with my life partner? It's been helpful and reminds me to assert myself in other settings as well. This journey with my husband is our own. I entered the marriage in large part to demonstrate to my parents how marriage should be. I wanted to show my dad that I could be treated well by a man, despite what he thought of me. My focus was off. How can someone truly have joy when they are living to prove someone else wrong? I am thankful God revealed this to me, that I needed to focus on the gifts he bestowed in my life. That he is the ultimate restorer of my faith and my relationship with my husband is not only a blessing to me, but can be to those around us.

I applied this work-to-earn mentality to my vision of God. I learned from my earthly father that the fruit of our labor comes from certain decisions. This is true; however, I never grasped the part that said he would love and support me regardless of the decision. Therefore, my view of God's grace was nonexistent. It wasn't until I learned what this meant that I could truly pursue my relationship with him, flaws and all. I started to understand, meaning I had head knowledge and my heart felt this, that God's love is not based on my behavior. Yeah, there are such things as natural consequences to my actions. But through it all, God loves and will bless me regardless because I'm his child and he already walked this day before me. I began applying this to my marriage more.

SIXTEEN

Self-Care Check-in

1. What does marriage and/or lifelong partnership mean to you? What roles should each partner play?
2. How do your DI symptoms impact your view of marriage and/or lifelong partnership? How do they affect your overall role in these relationships?
3. What moments do you find yourself projecting your DI symptoms onto your partner? For example, do you become irritable when they ask you a question? Lean into what that emotion (s) is (are); what do you tell yourself?

Activity:

It is important to be familiar with the connection between a trigger, thoughts, and emotions. When something happens, we are activated. This Activating event fires off a host of automatic thoughts that are rooted in core Beliefs. Then, there are Consequences, which include our emotional and behavioral responses. This process is called the ABC model.

It's time to take notes on what your patterns are so we can work to challenge them and break the negative cycle. Keep a record of your thoughts with this table below, which is based on REBT (Rational Emotive Behavioral Therapy).

Activating Event
Belief (automatic thoughts)
Consequences
Something Happens (Trigger)
I say to myself.
I feel. I do.

I saw my ex today.
He looks so good. How do I look? Will he try to talk to me? Am I tripping? He's married. So am I? Oh, goodness, I remember the time he and I...

Flustered. Anxious. Embarrassed. Hopeful. Reminiscent. Guilty.

*Refer to the feelings wheel for more emotions.

SEVENTEEN

DI and Motherhood

April 20, 2010 was a day for the books. I was working from home. It was sunny outside. There I was, watching The Fresh Prince of Bel-Air reruns while I answered customer concerns about their car payments. I hadn't felt right for a few days; my cycle was late and my anxiety had been high ever since. Especially because Aunt Flow was always on time to the party. As it so happened, I had a pregnancy test from the month before because I thought something was off then too.

I kept my concerns from Tony because I wasn't sure how he would react to being a father. Although we had been happy for years now, we hadn't spoken seriously about our futures. I was 25 years old with a good job, a car, and an apartment. Ya girl was living the dream. Tony was in his prime too, having held down a good job himself with his own apartment, car, and his best asset: me. It would be terrible timing to shake things up with a baby! Needless to say, I was grateful for the negative test in March 2010.

So, this sunny April day rolled along normally. I went about my routine when something told me to take the second pregnancy test. I figured it couldn't hurt--it would likely be negative too. I took a quick lunch break, peed on the stick and BAM: there were two lines. I immediately called my supervisor in a panic.

"I. HAVE. TO GOOOOOOOO," I cried. I was inconsolable.

"What's wrong, Christian?" my supervisor asked. I am quite sure she was going to call 911 and have them come to my house.

"I. Just took...a pregnancy test. It's positive," I wailed. It was even more upsetting to say out loud. I couldn't believe it.

After calming me down, my supervisor told me to take the day off and the next day too. She wouldn't let me get off the line until I was able to speak coherently and she was convinced I wouldn't harm myself.

I was home alone. Michele was at work and I didn't have anyone to call. I thought of my mother, but she was also at work. Plus, I couldn't call her until I was sure this wasn't a fluke. My thought spirals took over. *What's Tony going to say? Will he stay with me? Will he leave me like my dad told me he would? Oh. My. God. My dad. What's he going to think? How will he take the news? Is he going to tell me he 'told me so?'*

I'm not even sure why I was concerned about what my father would think. By this point, he and I hadn't spoken in three years. He still refused to take the paternity test or be part of my life. This was still a hold he had over me. I wondered how to gain his approval even then. I missed having him around, despite the fact that I knew our relationship wasn't healthy.

This is what happens when a relationship doesn't end in a mutually respectful manner. The last thing I said to him was probably "fuck you" after I made an attempt to reconnect two years into our mutual silence toward each another.

I flashed back to when I was graduating college in December 2008. It was by far the grandest accomplishment of my life up until then. Despite the disagreements he and I had, I wanted my father there. Naively, I was sure he wanted to be supportive of his only daughter. I sent him an email to break the ice, giving him the date, time, and location. He had all the information he needed to be present. He had the opportunity to be there for me and get to know who I was and be a part of who I was becoming. My invitation was an olive branch and something I hoped would be a clean slate for us.

A few days later, he wrote back: he turned down my invitation. It was heartbreaking. I had said all the right things, invited his wife and told him I was excited to see him. But he told me 'no.' How dare I send him an invitation in an email, he ranted, saying it wasn't the proper way to reach out. He had missed the entire point. That moment helped me realize who I was dealing with and where we stood. Moreover, I could see that he was stuck and not ready to move on with me. I knew it would take something huge for me to contact him again. A major event would have to happen before I subjected myself to the humiliation and unwelcome surprise of his own issues impacting me.

Welp, now the major thing had happened: a whole baby. Ugh! I had a chance to give him something he couldn't possibly refuse: a grandchild. I knew Daddy would disapprove on some level, but I felt drawn to share the information. I still wanted to have him back in my life. That was the trauma bonding again, wh

ere I thought subjecting myself to his emotional turmoil was preferable to not having him in my life.

I was embarking on one of the most powerful journeys of my life, motherhood. And I thought of calling my dad. My thought spirals were all over the place, mostly because I felt like the little girl who had done something wrong instead of celebrating. This is where it is important to examine the scripts from our family of origins. I was concerned about calling him to apologize for getting pregnant before marriage. I was robbing myself of joy because of what my father always said around me about other women and what he expected of me. I really had no idea how he would react. But the point to note is how powerful our insecurities are and how they can drive us to miss out on things that could be a true blessing.

I will never forget the six positive pregnancy tests I took on April 20, 2010. Between the four home tests, the STAT blood work and the urine sample I gave at a crisis pregnancy center, it was official: I was going to be a mommy. Thankfully, I wasn't alone. Michele came straight from work when she got my text. I was surrounded by her and Sauls, my other good friend who brought the four home tests from the Dollar Tree. My friends were in as much disbelief as I was. They had run the streets with me; we all knew this meant no more partying or shenanigans.

The time finally came for me to talk to Tony. He worked 10-hour shifts in a warehouse at the time and took a break at 7 p.m. every night.

"What's up, babe," Tony asked. Poor guy was not ready for what I had to tell him. I was so nervous. I hadn't even planned how to share the news.

"Umm, I took a pregnancy test. And it was positive," I told him after a beat of silence. I started crying.

"You straight?" He asked. Just as calm as he could be. I could tell he wasn't shaken. It made me feel more at ease.

"I don't know if I want to be pregnant," I confessed. "What do you think?"

"Well. I guess I gotta take care of you and a baby," he told me. Just like that, he was resolved and so was I. We were going to be parents.

After telling me everything would be ok and that he would see me that weekend, we ended the call. And I probably breathed for the first time since getting the news that day.

I have to say it: I don't really do kids. This was one of the humps I had to get over after dealing with my hang-ups about my dad and being an unwed mom. I just wasn't sure I could be a mother. There's a certain level of patience required to deal with the very spirit of a child that I knew I didn't have.

My mom was and still is one of the most selfless people I know. She would give me her last and figure her own stuff out later. When I was a child, I knew she loved me unconditionally because she showed it. I could talk to her about things when I was a teenager because she made me feel comfortable enough to share. She tried. And the effort meant a lot to both my brother and me. I knew I wanted to be a mom like her, one who would create a safe space for her children.

She partied a lot when she and Daddy split, and this was the side of motherhood that made me nervous. I wondered sometimes if my brother and I stressed her out so much that she had to leave sometimes. She was clearly trying to reclaim lost time from taking care of us and trying to nurture a doomed marriage. *Is this the kind of mother I would be? The kind that would be so stressed out that I would leave my kids up to their own devices as soon as they were old enough?* Here I was again, criticizing myself before I gave myself a chance to try. I saw my mother's nerves shot. And I watched Daddy push her buttons. He often judged her overtly so my brother and I would hear his disappointment in how she handled things.

The pressure was on while I was pregnant. I wanted to be the best mom, even better than my own so Tony wouldn't be disappointed in me about my parenting style. I didn't want that stress on our relationship. I was on a mission to create the perfect family. Clearly, it wasn't going to come from examples I'd known. So, I felt left to figure out motherhood on my own. I set up house. Surely the kid would need a place to stay that was warm and inviting. I was living an hour away from home, in my college town. I didn't plan to leave, but Tony expressed his commitment to me and the baby. He wanted to be a full-time father, so he asked me to move back home.

I was nervous about this step. It meant I had to move away from my best friend. We had been roommates for years at that point. I felt guilty for leaving Michele yet excited for a chance to build something new with my future husband. It was a next-level move. I was on my way to having the family I wanted so badly. I had a chance to recreate what a healthy, happy childhood should have been for someone.

As I prepared for our son, I commuted to work an hour away, learned to cook, read mom blogs, and consulted with other mothers, mine included. I even started going back to church. I mentioned this earlier. I knew I needed a connection to my Heavenly Father if I was going to get through this, especially since I had gone the first six months of my pregnancy without talking to the father who raised me. I was desperately trying to control everything around me.

With my tendency to be more anxiously attached to Tony, I found myself seeking approval from him in regards to my changing body and overall attitude. I wondered what kind of father he would be. *Will we agree on how to parent our son? What if he is like my own dad and doesn't validate our kid?! I won't have it.* I found myself in defensive mode quite early. I was faced with the perceived threat of living with a man who may actually turn out to be like my father. He hadn't given me the inkling that he was, but I'd heard too many times how living with someone changes people. This perceived threat to my emotional safety sparked a few arguments. But we managed. Looking back, it was a natural anxiety we had about the whole thing.

I eventually got tired of the silence between my dad and me. It was eating me up inside that I had not heard from him when he knew about the baby. I was at the shop getting my hair done one afternoon when my grandmother told me the news had gotten back to him that I was pregnant. It hurt that he didn't call, but I shouldn't have been surprised. I was clearly still the child in our relationship, a philosophy that many older generations subscribe to regarding who "should" initiate amends after a disagreement.

I was insecure about approaching him after such a long time. It had not been a whole three and a half years since we had a conversation. There was a failed attempt in between. The pressure I put on myself was fierce. I was scared and had no idea what I would say or how he would take the news coming from me.

I was six months pregnant, driving back from visiting a friend when I was hit with a sudden boldness. I decided to take the leap.

"Hey, Daddy. It's Christian," I said.

He laughed. "I know who it is," he said. I was shocked. He actually cared enough to save my information even after the hurtful things I said. The so-called disrespect hadn't turned him off as much as I thought. I guess he didn't really have to answer the phone call.

"So," I began awkwardly, "I'm having a baby."

"I heard," he said. It was uncomfortable. I'm sure none of us knew where to go next.

"I don't know if you remember Tony. He is the father," I told him. "It's a boy. We are going to name him Karter, with a 'K', to honor Tony's dad," I told him.

I couldn't help but throw a little sauce on that last statement. I wanted him to know a few things: I was still completely in love and loved by the man he told me would leave me. And we were having a baby. Despite the many words I had for my dad, I simply told him I wanted him to know his grandson.

"Well, let's meet soon, then," he said. There was not yet an ounce of disdain or disapproval in his voice. I guess babies really do change everything.

"Ok! I'm driving back from Rock Hill now. But I can meet for breakfast if you want," I replied. It was suddenly easier for me to have a conversation. He was accepting and appeared excited to hear from me.

We agreed to meet me at some point that week. I must admit, that reunion was amazing. The focus was on me, the baby, and the unforgettable Lizards Thicket breakfast! It's a staple restaurant in our town, where you can go feel like your southern grandmother is in the kitchen serving you the best bacon, eggs, and grits you have ever tasted. Daddy and I met for about an hour while he stared at me--my belly mostly. He was so nice and attentive. I could tell he missed me and I know he knew how I felt. It was a preview of how life could be if we could just get it together. I had hope that I had accomplished something for my unborn son. It was a good start to setting up his childhood; I was a good mom already.

That day was a spark of a new beginning for my dad and me. We were on a new trajectory. We talked daily, catching up on things. We knew we had to talk about "it", the paternity issue, but I don't think either of us really wanted to ruin what we found. Our relationship was never one that I would describe as close. I was too afraid to bring him certain things as a kid or teenager. But this was new. I was an adult and we both seemed to be getting into a good stride. I was a little bolder with my opinions. I told him I was hurt by him skipping my graduation. He told me he didn't want to mess up my day by being there. I'm not convinced that's valid.

I had found my voice, having been with Tony for years by then. It was refreshing to speak about things I wasn't allowed to back in the day, but I still held my tongue on certain subjects. This was all in the name of keeping the peace. I avoided bringing up the fact that I was being poked and prodded at weekly doctor visits toward the end of my pregnancy with a huge question in the back of my mind about who my father was. I wanted to get the answer once and for all. But I didn't think I was valuable enough to know. I sacrificed this knowledge and continued to answer medical family history questions with half of the truth.

Karter came into the world. The annoying labor experience was no indication of how wonderful he is. Daddy came to the hospital and visited. He saw his grandson. I wondered if he had any ill-feelings toward my new baby. I wanted to know if he truly felt connected given the still unaddressed paternity issue. But my dad was absolutely smitten. Throughout Karter's life, my dad has been present, supportive, and proud. We coasted through the years post-"it" like a breeze. At least it seemed that way.

Occasionally, I struggled with the symptoms of my DI. Self-doubt would creep in, starting with the feeling that our reunion was too good to be true. When would the other shoe drop? When was the right time to talk about the hurt and embarrassment? How would we truly address the disrespect and disregard we both had toward one another? Like anyone who doesn't want to deal with the root issue, we brushed it away.

I loved talking to him about adult things several times a day. I enjoyed his feedback and hearing him say he was impressed by me, which was rare in our relationship. When I was a kid, I didn't get validation. No matter how well I did in school or in the band or managing to graduate with no babies! It's possible he thought I didn't need it because I accomplished enough without him and was therefore alright. He was wrong. It made me strive harder for his attention and approval and this carried over into my parenting.

The decisions I made with my son were partly based on whether I was going to make my dad proud. I was raising my son with Tony, but I had that same loop in the back of my head. *What would Daddy do? Is he going to judge me for not doing this or that?* I think many people have their parents' voices stuck in their heads, judging them on their childrearing. It was strong in my case. I dealt with this on top of being a new mother with no experience with babies--even babysitting gigs as a teen. I had trouble standing my ground on some decisions, partially due to balancing having my dad back in my life and keeping Tony assured he was my Number One partner in this new phase of our relationship.

For a woman with DI, self-doubt is amplified. Some of the decisions I made about our son annoyed my husband because he thought I was trying to parent to get my father's attention. He was right: I continued to grasp for approval and this was just a new way to do it. I had to learn that Tony was indeed the father, that I wasn't raising our kid with my dad. Even if my father was coming from a good place it sounded like a commandment. It took a lot of work to find a balance of different opinions between the two of them, especially when raising a son.

Tony and I decided not to spank our kids. I didn't want to subject our son to what I saw my father do to my brother. I knew it wasn't effective, unless you're trying to scare your kid and drive a wedge between you. When I shared this part of our parenting style with my dad, he scoffed.

"Humph," he said. "You already know if he comes over here and acts up, I don't play that."

"Ok, I know," I said blandly, even though I was screaming inside.

Where was the moxy I learned over the years of silence? I had finally learned to use my voice, but was too afraid to use it. It was so hard for me to just tell him it was unacceptable to put his hands on my son per our guidelines. I reverted back to the obedient child who asked no questions. It didn't matter that I was the mother.

Motherhood thus far taught me a lot about myself. This is what happens in any type of relationship: the other person acts as a mirror to show us parts of ourselves we didn't know were there. Our kids bring out the inner child in us. We are in a position to relearn things we forgot, such as the clean slate we held about the people and the world around us before our worldviews were shaped into what they are now. If we have been conditioned to notice the ugly parts of the world after years of being disappointed, it will certainly come out in our parenting. The following are only a few of the types of mothers and are obviously co-occurring with other issues, but let's talk about how their DI plays a role.

The 'Best Friend' Mom

Wanting to be your child's confidant can come from the best place. It's amazing how some women create a safe environment for their children to turn to when they have issues. I consider myself a friendly mother. However, it is easy to get caught up in the good parts of motherhood in this regard. There is a line we sometimes forget about when it comes to parenting our children.

Remember Keisha from the Friendship chapter of this book? She was the 'Needy Friend' who didn't like new people invading her established relationships. Her idea of friendship meant she was the priority. Otherwise, she questioned loyalties and felt insecure because her inner narrative shouted she wasn't good enough to keep friends around. She and I tapped into her role as a mother. She gave her son mostly everything he wanted, to the detriment of her partner. The child knew he could depend on Keisha because she proved to be the reliable friend she hoped she would have one day. They had open communication and she was supportive of him. She met his needs and made sure to fulfill as many wants as possible. It wasn't hard for her to meet her own standard in this regard because she had a chance to raise the friend she wanted to have.

"Since he got older and all his 'lil friends come over, I don't get no time," Keisha said disapprovingly.

"Seems like you're hurt. I wonder if you considered how natural it is for him to forge his own relationships," I reflected.

Keisha had done some work. She knew the void her father left informed her neediness; however, she couldn't give up the chance to recreate the childhood she wanted, including the friendships she wanted. Her concerns as a parent were typical. For the mother who is bonded in a healthy way to her children, it is certainly an adjustment to accept the shift in the relationship dynamics. It can be tough.

This is where we have to make sure we are constantly in tune with our triggers. For Keisha, it was important for her to understand the negative relationship she had with her father and how it impacted her interpretation of her son making friends.

The 'Helicopter' Mom

You may be familiar with this woman. She is the mother who keeps her children within her sight at all times. She continuously checks in with her child, making sure their needs are met. There is also the extreme case of the HM who may as well keep her child in a bubble! She is highly attentive, sometimes overly so, and is usually referred to as overbearing. It's rare that this woman allows her child much freedom.

This anxiously attached mother is doing what she knows how to do best: control. Anxiety has us believe we do not have dominion of anything around us or anything inside us. It's especially scary for a mother who is tasked with helping another person survive the world she has not yet figured out herself.

This woman must be in charge. She is much like the HWIC friend we talked about earlier. Her attitude about relationships is about keeping things status quo according to her standards only, as it helps her feel more at ease.

Recall Mary, the 'Clingy' girlfriend from the Friendship chapter who had to know her partner's location at all times. She was sexually abused by her father, which gave her a warped view of her physical and emotional safety around men. If not checked, her mentality about the world could impact her mothering. Her habits could easily morph into a lingering, needy parent. While completely valid to want to keep your children safe, you must check the motivation of all behavior: Is the helicopter mom's intention tied to fear?

The 'Perfectionist' Mom

I can relate to this style of parenting. It stems from the anxious attachment style, where I found myself performing to keep the attention of my husband and my father before him. I found myself checking in with my son during his first few years, asking if I was doing a good job and what I needed to change to be better. This is actually a good skill to have as a partner in any relationship, especially a parenting relationship. But, if I'm honest, those questions were coming from a different place: insecurity. I had a warped idea that my son would leave me. I had already been left by my father, I told myself, because I wasn't good enough to keep him around.

I was confronted with my own issues the more I interacted with my son. Having two boys now is even more triggering at times. Perfectionism shows up in different ways for me. As a new mother, I found how this related to my people-pleasing mentality. I wanted to present the perfect product, be it dinner, laundry, gifts, quality time, etc. If it wasn't met with the highest praise I would be offended and lash out. That looked like yelling at the family or myself. I would rant about how much work I put into something and it wasn't good enough. I had forgotten that a child's palate doesn't always appreciate a tender steak; Spaghettios are just fine for a three-year-old!

Perfectionism. Performing. People pleasing. It all goes hand-in-hand for this type of mother. The quality of a task for her child means a lot to her, as it has been intertwined with her self worth. In order to break this cycle, we must begin by exploring where we learned this message. If it is indeed mostly related to the paternal relationships, or lack thereof, the work begins with separating yourself from the mistakes of the father. Removing the blame is crucial for healing. It is time to identify with who you are.

Motherhood. It's what you make it. I've made some strange decisions. But I can say without a shadow of a doubt I'm an awesome mom. My kids are my world. I live by the common theme of wanting to do better than both my parents. As a woman with DI, that can go to the extreme. There are moments when I specifically have my dad in my head when I make decisions. I wonder if it's something he would do, so I can ensure it's done the "right" way. My dad comes out when I speak sometimes, which means things can come out ugly. Then I feel remorseful. The cycle can be relentless if I let it.

The point of grace is we keep it moving and remain thankful for new mercies. I have my DI to thank for my mothering, as well. Because of the symptoms that arise, I am more aware of when I need to be gentle. That I can still have respect when I apologize for being ugly. I am open to having conversations about many things and encourage a safe space. I use the myriad of examples that God shares with us in his word about the relationships he has with his children. He's stern, yet loving. Patient, but sets expectations for our conduct. It's helpful. I know my children are his and try to be a good steward over his gifts to me.

My dad and I had our final blow-up two years before the manuscript of this book was complete. The same issue reared its head. I have to say, it was more than the fact he didn't take the paternity test. The more I sat with the anger, I understood it to be hurt, disappointment, embarrassment, invalidation. There are more things I discovered about my sentiments that I believe became evident after becoming a mother. I started learning who I am and the type of person I wanted to be. My new self would encompass a whole person who would be awesome despite what he made me feel.

I am free. And I am ready to share with you how I got here.

EIGHTEEN

Self-Care Check-in

1. If you are a mother, or a mother figure, what have you learned about yourself?
2. Our children usually don't mean any harm, especially at a younger age. But that doesn't mean the things they say and do don't strike a chord. Think of the first time your child told you "no." What did that activate for you? What thoughts or feelings did you notice?
3. Perhaps you have decided not to have children, or you were unable to for some reason. Think about how your DI symptoms interact with this decision, nondecision, and/or inability regarding parenthood, given what you took from your own FOO.

Activity:

Write a letter to your mother or mother figure. Maybe she was your biological mother, grandmother, aunt, or trusted friend of the family. Tell her how your DI symptoms have impacted you. Educate her on what you learned about yourself in order to help her realize hers. What would you suggest she needs for healing?

NINETEEN

Overcoming Daddy Issues

By now, you know my story. It's been quite the journey. I'm grateful it's not done yet. In fact, it feels like a new beginning ever since I've accepted some truths about living with Daddy Issues for so long. I've shown you how DI can show up across the spectrum and how it evolves if not managed properly.

YOU'VE ALSO PUT in the work. You've reflected. And hopefully, you realized the need to take your self-care seriously and started a journey toward healing of your own. It's your time to experience freedom too! Introspection is vital to this process. Let's remind ourselves of where we started. What are Daddy Issues?

Diagnostic Criteria

1. *The physical and/or emotional absence to*

overbearing physical and/or emotional presence of a
father that results in at least one of the following:

2. Feelings and/or thoughts of abandonment
3. Feelings and/or thoughts of worthlessness
4. Confusion and/or difficulty making decisions
5. The presence of a father where the relationship was
   unhealthy. This may result in one or more of the
   following:
6. Extreme stress
7. Inability to trust one's own judgment
8. Feelings and/or thoughts of inadequacy
9. The person has experienced consistent trouble
   manifesting healthy relationships.This applies to
   familial, professional, intimate, and parenting
   relationships (must appear in at least one of these
   categories).
10. The doubt, shame, abandonment, anxiety, and/or
    depression is persistent to some degree, lasting at
    least 6 weeks in children and adolescents and at least
    3 months for adults.
11. The disturbance causes clinically significant distress
    in multiple areas of one's life, evident in one's
    behavior.

ONE THING IS FOR SURE: a diagnosis is not always a
permanent condition. Just like cancer symptoms can alleviate
and enter remission, so can the symptoms of DI! There's
hope in this process of healing. We shall overcome!

· · ·

NOW, WHAT DO I MEAN "OVERCOME?" My interpretation is that you can think of something hurtful and it doesn't send that negative, overwhelming emotional charge down your spine. You are an overcomer when you are not activated by an unhealthy level of anxiety--the kind that keeps you up at night, worrying about how life would have been if you ____. You know you've overcome something when you can pinpoint how you dealt with the negative emotional, mental, physical, and spiritual hang-ups. You've found who and what you need when symptoms decrease. You acknowledge your strengths at the other side of things. You don't beat yourself up for feeling the negativity. Instead, you spend your energy pouring into yourself. Maybe you found a way to help others through their journey as they watched you.

THIS PROCESS IS ONGOING. It requires regular check-ins to catch the inevitable setbacks. This process is also individualized. You will need to decide what you want to address first. Do you tackle the spiraling thoughts in the beginning? Do you kick the butt of Negative Nancy in your head? Yes, sis. Use the power you forgot you had. Or, discover the strength that was there all along. We are only human, so it's important to pace ourselves and find reasons to love us through the journey. You must intentionally take your time on the moving parts before you miss something crucial. Again, this process looks different for everyone. However, I have an original guide on how to apply GRACE to every situation.

GET TO KNOW YOUR SYMPTOMS.

I can't stress this enough! It is crucial to know where you currently stand so your steps can be ordered properly. The DI symptoms are listed above. Ask yourself: *How do these symptoms look in my life?* This will help guide you through the first part of the self-awareness process, where you get to know how these symptoms manifest. What do you tell yourself about your sense of self-worth, for instance? How does this feel in your body? How do you emotionally respond when you think of yourself? How was the message created? Who helped build your self-worth and who threatened it? How does your behavior impact others?

YOU CAN ALSO ASK people who know you well what they notice about you as a friend, a wife, a mother, a human being! Objective views are helpful in that they offer insight we miss. Not good with words? Draw your feelings about the symptoms. Use a song to describe your thoughts and feelings about the insight you have. Pray, asking God to reveal the ugly so he can clean it up. Whatever you need to do to be able to articulate your findings, do it...in a healthy, loving way of course.

Rescript *the negative messages you learned.*

Everything we learned is from someone else. Period. We pick up our knowledge by watching others carry out their daily lives. We talked about the family of origin, which impacts us 100 percent of the time. Once you learn how your DI symptoms manifest, it's time to explore where your self-talk came from and how it contributes to this condition. Who taught you the things you tell yourself? Which messages stand out as the most hurtful? The most impactful? The negative messages you learned from your father's presence and/or absence directly influence our scripts. However, we have to consider the DI symptoms of the people who raised us and how their own messages were passed down to us.

YOU HAVE the power to rescript every unhealthy message. You have the power to eradicate the power it seems to have over you. Ever thought, *I can't trust others?* That's a common core belief women with DI symptoms have. You can challenge this message by reworking that into a more rational solution: *There are trustworthy people.* Everyone is not out to harm us. That's a fact. We forget over time the level of trust we used to have for others. It gets clouded by the pain we experience in relationships, especially from paternal trauma. However, I am hoping you can come up with examples to negate the lies. Following the trust example, think of someone you have been able to trust, even if it was just to do a small favor such as hand you a pen, take you to dinner, answer your phone call. Boom! You've already found a plot hole in the story you made up in your head.

Address your self-care needs.

You have great tools in this book to help kickstart your self-care regimen. Now that you are familiar with how DI symptoms affect you and the root of the messages are clear, you can focus on tuning into what those messages are pointing you to. For instance, if the message you learned from childhood was "You're not good enough," and you found that to be linked to a feeling of inadequacy, then you likely tried to fill the void with a slew of things. It may have been alcohol or drug use, sleeping with people without regard for your own safety or health, or other reckless behavior. Your soothing behavior may have been to stay busy, resembling the overachieving, perfectionist personality we discussed earlier. Either way, these actions help in the moment. They help us forget the nagging "not good enough" loop. If your behavior is masking insecurity, then seek an activity to reinforce your confidence. Develop a self-care routine that is not overwhelming, yet does just enough to challenge the lies you've told yourself.

Connect *with others who uplift you.*

Shame cannot live in community. This is something I learned from author Brene Brown, mentioned earlier in this book. Anxiety and insecurity will have us believe we are bad people and shouldn't share our flaws with anyone else. This is not accurate. It's not grace. Connecting with other people who have also experienced difficult times is what helps us survive. In fact, belonging is a crucial part of the hierarchy of needs, a list of things Maslow gave us to prioritize the things we need to survive.

THE #MeToo and the #BlackLivesMatter Movements are great examples of connection. They exist to connect people who don't feel seen or heard. The main goal is to offer a platform for voices that have been stamped out for years. How do you think your voice has been stamped out? Who can you connect with on a smaller scale to feel validated? It is also worth mentioning the disconnect we have within ourselves. For survivors of trauma, it is especially difficult to feel at one with the mind and body, as disassociation (the body's attempt to detach from reality) is a primary defense mechanism when one feels threatened. Yoga, meditation, dance and/or movement is great for reconnecting one's mind with the body in a safe way.

Enforce proper boundaries.

I heard that "no" is a complete sentence once. It is something I am getting better at with practice. Once you know what people, places and things activate the negative feelings in you, use those feelings as clues. Lean into those emotions and listen to their direction; it's likely that they are telling you to run! Your mental, spiritual, emotional, and physical health depend on this very thing.

IS your relationship with chocolate ice cream too tight? Think of your sugar levels! Ask yourself: Do I use this as my main source of comfort? What am I running from? Who is triggering me enough to run to my ice cream? Is it really worth my physical health to eat so much of it? You may believe this to be a silly example, but it's true: our mental health and physical health play off one another. The reciprocal impact between the two can offer a clue about where to set a hard line.Once you sit with it, you may find that it's time to make a change in a certain relationship because it is too toxic. We can become bitter, expecting our offenders to be affected by the poison we are drinking.

WHAT IS CLOSURE?

As I write this book, my father and I do not speak. In fact, I tried to reach out, but my efforts were not enough. I started to see the way my efforts to correct things impacted me. My family suffered when I wasn't as present as I wanted to be due to my preoccupation with my dad. I had to realize the connection that mattered was the one with my Heavenly

Father. I did my work. By finding his loving grace, I am alright with me and excited for my future.

NOW, about closure. I'm ready to address this myth, that closure is reliant on the other party. I believe we can have rest. Peace is definitely within reach as long as we are willing to acknowledge we need work, which largely involves us cleaning up our own acts. The more we can bravely lean into ourselves, relying on our God-given power, and pour into healthy relationships, the more we can let go.

WE CAN ACHIEVE closure for ourselves. It is not true that we need the offending, Earthly Father to truly find peace. That puts way too much power in their hands. There is too much life to lose when we concern ourselves with the approval of another person. If we focus on closing anything, it should be the door that leads to the thoughts driving our insecurities, self-doubt, and feelings of worthlessness. We close the door on our DI symptoms and open that path that leads to healing. As we uplift ourselves, we give back that love we missed from our earthly fathers to our sisters and our brothers. It's part of the formula that points to our Heavenly Father. Of course, this is freedom for me. How will it look in your life?

TWENTY

Self Care Check-in

Alright, sis. We've been on quite a journey together. Perhaps you've made some connections you never considered or you finally decided to stop and do the work. Let's check in on that promise you made to yourself in the beginning of this book. How's that self-care plan going?

I have improved my **mental** health by doing the following things on my list:

I know I am better because [insert ways you know you are different-[e.g. I cut that relationship off, etc.]
I can do more...
I will know I keep making strides by...[e.g. I'm talking more positively to myself, etc.]
I deserve a treat! By next week I will [insert reward]

I have improved my **physical** health by doing the following things on my list:

I know I am better because [insert ways you know you are different, e.g. I started going for walks, etc.]
I can do more...
I will know I keep making strides by...[e.g. the fact that I have less junk food in my pantry, etc.]
I deserve a treat! By next week I will [insert reward]

I have improved my **emotional** health by doing the following things on my list:

I know I am better because [insert ways you know you are different, e.g. I cried with a friend, etc.]
I can do more...
I will know I keep making strides because...[e.g. I started voicing my emotions in important relationships, etc.]
I deserve a treat! By next week I will [insert reward]

I have improved my **spiritual** health by doing the following things on my list:

I know I am better because [insert ways you know you are different, e.g. I started talking to God more, etc.]
I can do more...
I will know I keep making strides because...[e.g. I started listening to Mike Todd sermons from Transformation Church, etc.]
I deserve a treat! By next week I will [insert reward]

A Letter from Christian

TO MY DEAREST SISTER,

I SEE YOU. I HEAR YOU. I CAN FEEL YOUR PAIN TO THE EXTENT THAT MY OWN EXPERIENCE ALLOWS. YOU HAVE BEEN HURT BY YOUR FATHER IN WAYS THAT ARE BEYOND VERBAL, EMOTIONAL, MENTAL, AND SPIRITUAL ABUSE. YOU SIS, MAY BE A SURVIVOR OF PHYSICAL AND/OR SEXUAL ASSAULT AT THE HANDS OF YOUR FATHER. HE IS SUPPOSED TO BE HERE TO PROTECT YOU, BUT HE DIDN'T. HE VIOLATED YOUR RIGHT TO YOUR BODY. AND THIS LEFT YOU FEELING LIKE YOU WERE DAMAGED.

YOU DON'T NECESSARILY WANT TO HEAR THAT YOU ARE A FIGHTER, THAT YOU ARE STRONGER AND HERE ON EARTH FOR A REASON. MAYBE YOU DON'T EVEN WANT TO SHARE YOUR STORY WITH OTHERS. IT'S YOUR CHOICE TO MAKE. IT IS ALSO YOUR CHOICE TO DECIDE TO LOOK FEAR IN THE FACE AND STAND UP TO IT. STARE AT THE DEPRESSION YOU DEVELOPED AFTER DEALING WITH THE CONSEQUENCES OF THE ABUSE AND SIT WITH IT. TURN IT ON ITS HEAD AND

TAKE YOUR POWER BACK. YOU HAVE THE OPPORTUNITY TO WRITE YOUR FUTURE. YOU GET TO DECIDE WHAT YOU NEED BECAUSE IT'S YOUR LIFE.

MANY OF OUR SISTERS FEEL THEY HAVE NO POWER. I SIT WITH THEM SEVERAL TIMES A WEEK IN MY OFFICE. THEY CAN'T SEE BEYOND THE PAIN, LIKE YOU. I HEAR THEIR HOPELESSNESS AND DISGUST. I SEE THE SHAME THEY FEEL. YOU KNOW WHAT? THAT SHAME IS A LIE. I HOPE READING THIS BOOK GIVES YOU THE COURAGE TO DO THE OPPOSITE OF WHAT YOU THINK YOU MAY WANT TO DO. IF YOU WANT TO STAY IN BED ALL DAY, DO SOMETHING DIFFERENT. YOU MAY BE PLEASANTLY SURPRISED BY WHERE IT LEADS YOU. THIS IS A LITTLE TRICK THAT HELPS SEVERELY DEPRESSED OR ANXIOUS PEOPLE SLOWLY TAKE BACK THEIR POWER. I CANNOT GIVE YOU POWER, INTENTION, OR PURPOSE. BUT I CAN LEAVE YOU WITH THE NOTION THAT FREEDOM IS POSSIBLE--TAKE IT FROM ME. I'VE SEEN WOMEN COME FROM THE DEEPEST, DARKEST PLACES AND WIN.

I ALSO KNOW YOU MAY NOT KNOW GOD. YOU MAY BE ANNOYED THAT I BRING HIM UP BECAUSE YOU CAN'T IMAGINE WHY HE WOULD ALLOW THOSE THINGS TO HAPPEN TO YOU. I GET IT. I AM AWARE OF SPIRITUAL ABUSE, WHERE AN AGGRESSOR USES GOD'S NAME TO DO UNSPEAKABLE THINGS. I'VE BEEN ASKED 'WHERE WAS HE WHEN...' ALL THE TIME. THERE'S NO SHORT ANSWER HERE. BUT ONE THING IS FOR SURE: MANY PEOPLE THINK THE SAME WAY, HAVING HAD SIMILAR EXPERIENCES. I'VE BEEN MAD AT GOD BEFORE. YOU ARE NOT ALONE AND YOU ARE NOT IMMUNE TO HIS GRACE, SHOULD YOU DECIDE YOU WANT TO EXPLORE A RELATIONSHIP WITH HIM. MY OWN JOURNEY LED ME TO HIM, BUT I UNDERSTAND IT MAY END UP TOTALLY DIFFERENT FOR YOU. THAT'S YOUR CHOICE. WHAT I WANT YOU TO WALK

AWAY WITH IS THE FACT THAT YOU HAVE OPTIONS. PERIOD. THE ABUSE YOU ENDURED WANTS YOU TO THINK YOU ARE POWERLESS AND HAVE NO VOICE. BUT THAT IS FALSE.

UNFORTUNATELY, YOU LIVE WITH THE CONSEQUENCES LIKE WE ALL DO, BUT WE DON'T HAVE TO STAY DOWN. MY HOPE IS YOU CHASE THE PATH THAT GIVES YOU PEACE. IF YOU HAPPEN TO BE RIDDLED WITH THESE HARD QUESTIONS, I CAN BE HERE FOR YOU. YOU ARE NOT ALONE.

LOVE,

S. CHRISTIAN JACKSON

About Christian

S. Christian Jackson, LPC, CACI, NCC

Christian Jackson is a Licensed Professional Counselor in the state of South Carolina. She also has her Certified Addictions Counselor credential, which helps her support people in recovery from drug and alcohol use using evidence-based practices. Her niche is trauma. As an EMDR (Eye-Movement Desensitization and Reprocessing) therapist, Christian is trained to take a unique dive into processing the implications of traumatic experiences. As she honed her skills in various capacities and roles, Christian embarked on a journey that would allow her to address gaps in treatment and education regarding mental health for almost a decade. Christian is co-owner of YANA Counseling Services, where she facilitates therapy and trains upcoming licensed professional counselors. As co-founder of JP Training SC, she facilitates professional development for agencies across the State, consults, and is booked for motivational speeches for various organizations regarding the impact of mental health issues, if left untreated and how to address them.

Christian is a wife, mother of two, and a good friend. She enjoys reading, writing, and binging her favorite shows on Netflix if she can find the time!